MICHELANGELO'S SCULPTURES
COMPLETE EDITION

Michelagniolo

ETCHING BY AN UNKNOWN MASTER · ABOUT 1560

THE SCULPTURES OF
MICHELANGELO

PHAIDON EDITION
OXFORD UNIVERSITY PRESS · NEW YORK

MADE IN GREAT BRITAIN

PRINTED BY HARRISON & SONS LTD · PRINTERS TO HIS MAJESTY THE KING · LONDON

FOREWORD

TO COME NEARER to the work of Michelangelo, the greatest sculptor of his millenary—that is what has been attempted in this volume. Natural sight is set against scientific sifting, ocular perception against the experience of historical and critical conceptions. The great art-historians of the preceding century, owing to the costliness of means of reproduction and the unnaturalistic transposition of all such representations, were compelled to present works of art by means of description. By thus transforming the visible and tangible into words, they appealed to the inner, not to the outer eye; but for this very reason every detail became clear, and all the context too; the description was at the same time an explanation, throwing light on that which they thought should be shown. The development of the processes of reproduction, which have become naturalistic in the course of the last fifty years, has increased the ocular knowledge of art research, but at the same time has replaced the selective analysis which verbal descriptions provided by barren surveys without spiritual details—summaries such as may be found in the items of an inventory. Only the photograph of the chosen detail in conjunction with a rendering of the whole in the proper light can provide an adequate equivalent for explanatory description; sometimes it can give more than words can ever give—an unequivocal representation of a definite view and an intimate insight into the working motions of the artist's tools. For this, however, an approximation to the actual dimensions and a considered arrangement of lighting are indispensable.

The catalogue which follows contains an epitome of the substance of old knowledge and conjecture concerning Michelangelo; the limited number of new conjectures it has been possible to include has been cautiously and indeed diffidently worded, and in most cases has been relegated to the notes.

Knowledge and opinion concerning the spiritual and technical foundations of Michelangelo's works; a guide and an aid to the eye, to the understanding and mental retention of them—all that will not hinder the reader from enjoying their full beauty with that freedom from predisposition with which all beauty should be enjoyed. For he who has knowledge of the phenomenon of the spectrum can enjoy the gleaming purity of sunlight not less than the child who accepts this gift as it accepts the miracle of its own life.

LONDON, WINTER 1939-40   LUDWIG GOLDSCHEIDER

The following catalogue contains so many references to the literature on Michelangelo that a separate bibliography would be superfluous. A list of the most important sources and biographies will be found in our volume devoted to Michelangelo's Paintings. In addition to these the following general works must be mentioned :—Adolf Philippi, Der Begriff der Renaissance, Leipzig 1912.—Francesco Flamini, Il Cinquecento, Milan 1898.—J. A. Symonds, The Renaissance in Italy, 5 vols., London 1877 f.—Karl Brandt, Die Renaissance in Florenz und Rom, 5th edition, Leipzig 1920.—Georg Voigt, Die Wiederbelebung des klassischen Altertums, 3rd edition, Berlin 1893.—Konrad Burdach, Reformation, Renaissance, Humanismus, Berlin 1918.—Arnaldo della Torre, Storia dell' Accademia Platonica di Firenze, Florence 1902.

LIST OF ABBREVIATED TITLES

Panofsky—Erwin Panofsky, Michelangelo-Literatur seit 1914. Jahrbuch für Kunstgeschichte, Vol. I, Vienna 1923.

Symonds—John Addington Symonds, The Life of Michelangelo Buonarroti, Vols. I and II, London 1893.

Thode—Henry Thode, Michelangelo und das Ende der Renaissance, 3 vols. (Vol. I, 1902 ; II, 1903 ; III, 1912).— Michelangelo, Kritische Untersuchungen, 3 vols. (Vol. I, 1908 ; II, 1908 ; III, 1913). The last three are referred to as Thode IV–VI.

Justi I—Carl Justi, Michelangelo, Beiträge zur Erklärung der Werke und des Menschen, Leipzig 1900.

Justi II—Carl Justi, Michelangelo, Neue Beiträge, Berlin, 1909.

Dvorak II—Max Dvořák, Geschichte der italienischen Kunst im Zeitalter der Renaissance, Akademische Vorlesungen, 3rd edition, 2 vols., Munich 1929.

Knapp—Fritz Knapp, Michelangelo, Klassiker der Kunst, 5th edition, Stuttgart n. d. (1925).

Mackowsky—Hans Mackowsky, Michelangelo, new edition, Berlin 1931.

Frey, Leben—Karl Frey, Michelangelo Buonarroti. Sein Leben und seine Werke, Vol. I (the other volumes have not been published), Berlin 1907.

Frey, Quellen—Karl Frey, Michelangelo Buonarroti. Quellen und Forschungen, Vol. I, Michelangelos Jugendjahre, Berlin 1907.

Brinckmann—A. E. Brinckmann, Barockskulptur, Handbuch der Kunstwissenschaft, Berlin 1917 f.

Wölfflin, Jugendwerke—Heinrich Wölfflin, Die Jugendwerke Michelangelos, Munich 1891.

Z.f.b.K.—Zeitschrift für bildende Kunst, Leipzig 1866 f.

MADONNA OF THE STAIRS. Plate 1 (2).

Marble relief, 22 × 15⅜ inches. First mentioned by Vasari in the second edition of his Lives (1568), and described by him as not quite a Florentine braccia[1] high and "the only bas-relief" by Michelangelo; according to Vasari it then belonged to Leonardo, Michelangelo's nephew. Leonardo gave it to the Medici, who presented it to the Casa Buonarroti in 1617.—Thode dates it 1490-1491; Knapp, 1493; Brinckmann, who assigns it to the Venetian period, 1494.—Attention has often been drawn, especially by Bode, to its relationship to reliefs by Donatello.—The attribution to Michelangelo has sometimes been disputed, without adequate grounds.

Wölfflin, Z.f.b.K. 1893, p. 108 f.—Courajod, Gazette des Beaux-Arts I, 1881, p. 199.—Symonds I, 29.—Frey, Quellen, p. 84 f.—Justi II, 32 f.—Thode III, 74 f.; IV, 10 f.—Bode, Florentiner Bildhauer, 4th edition, pp. 174 and 318.—Brinckmann, p. 18.—Panofsky, col. 12.

THE RAPE OF DEJANIRA. Plate 4 (3, 5, 6, 7).

Marble relief, 31⅛ × 34⅝ inches.—Vasari (1568) calls it "a fight between Hercules and the Centaurs", following Condivi, who in 1553 described it as "the Rape of Dejanira and the battle of Centaurs". According to Condivi, the idea of this relief was suggested to Michelangelo by Poliziano (1454-1494), the tutor of Lorenzo de' Medici's sons. The poet and humanist Poliziano perhaps derived his knowledge of the subject from Boccaccio's Genealogy (in the later Paris edition of 1511, Book IX, 29 f.) or from the collection of legends attributed to Hyginus (fabula 31). Here it is related how Hercules appeared at the wedding of Dejanira and the Cyclopean king Eurytion, in order to carry off the bride, who had previously been betrothed to him.—In view of Condivi's clear statement that the rape of *Dejanira* is represented, it is merely causing needless confusion to try and interpret it as a rape of Deidameia (Ovid, Metam. XII).—The individual figures in this relief have little material distinctness; it is hard to decide which are Centaurs, and still more difficult to distinguish males from females. Wölfflin maintained that there were no female figures in the relief, whereas Symonds believed that the central figure was female. According to Justi, however, this central figure is the Centaur Eurytus, according to Knapp it is Hercules or Theseus. The representation is modelled on sarcophagus fronts of the Roman Imperial period, and Bertoldo's equestrian relief has rightly been compared with it. Michelangelo seems to have been very fond of his Dejanira relief (this is confirmed by Condivi); in any case he kept it all his life and it then passed into the possession of his family.

Hyginus, Munkerus edition, Amsterdam 1681; "Fabulæ", Schmidt edition, 1872, fab. 31 (129, 171, 174).—Justi II, 22 f.—Frey, Leben, 96 f.; Quellen, 82 f.—Thode III, 77 f.; IV, 8 f.—Wölfflin, Jugendwerke, 1891, p. 10 f.—Symonds I, 27 f.—Brinckmann, p. 13 f.—Wickhoff, Die Antike im Bildungsgange Michelangelos, Mitteilungen d. Inst. f. österreichische Geschichtsforschung II, Innsbruck 1882.—Strzygowski, Jahrbuch d. preussischen Kunstsamml. XII, No. 4, 1891.—A. Hekler, Michelangelo und die Antike, Wiener Jahrb. f. Kunstgesch., Vol. VII, p. 203.—Johannes Wilde, Mitt. d. Kunsthist. Inst. in Florenz, 1932, IV, p. 48 f.

THE THREE BOLOGNA STATUETTES. Plates 8, 9 and 16 (10-15).

Marble, 27½ to 31½ inches high. Condivi mentions only the *Petronius* and the *Angel holding a candlestick* and says that Michelangelo was paid eighteen ducats[2] for the saint and twelve for the angel. The *Proculus*, "the most interesting of the three figures" (Johannes Wilde), is first mentioned, together with the two other sculptures, by Leandro Alberti in 1535 in his "De Divi Dominici abitu et sepultura". "Foratti disputes the authenticity of the Proculus, which it is true one would not be sorry to see eliminated from Michelangelo's works, but which is too well authenticated by Lodovico da Pelormo[3] and Leandro Alberti to justify its rejection without other reasons" (Panofsky). In addition to Foratti, Wölfflin and Frey have declared themselves against the attribution of the Proculus to Michelangelo, while Thode, Mackowsky, and Bode have given the best reasons for this attribution. According to contemporary reports the statue was knocked down and broken in 1572 while it was being cleaned. The shanks were broken off and it is still easy to see where they were stuck on again.—Apart from the question of authenticity, there is a sharp conflict of opinion as to the Proculus. Justi: "A plain-looking youth with a thick head and common features. . . . The small squinting eyes send forth sinister and cunning glances." Thode, on the other hand: "In my opinion there can be no doubt that in the Proculus we have a self-portrait of the nineteen-year-old artist. The shape of the forehead, the puckered wrinkles between the eyebrows, the widely placed eyes, the nose injured by Torrigiano's blow, the powerful lines running from the nose to the mouth, the shape of the lips with their drawn-in corners, the plump cheeks—all the features agree with his later portraits. His personality speaks to us directly and with animation. . . . If we consider him in this way, we get quite a different idea

---

[1] 23 inches.

[2] The purchasing power of a ducat in modern currency would be about £5. Michelangelo thus received about £150 for the two sculptures.

[3] Custodian of the Arca of San Domenico, Bologna, from 1527. His chronicle is said to have been begun in 1530. (Ricordi, quoted in Fanfani's Spigolature Michleangelesche, p. 152.)

of the saintly boy: he seems to be an improvisation, like a self-avowal of the young artist, caught from a momentary glimpse in the mirror and transfixed in stone". (*See* Plate 11.) Where so much is doubtful, it is permissible to question whether this little figure is worth so much argument.—Justi's opinion of the *Petronius* is harsh: "It seems hardly worth while discussing this indifferent and tasteless statuette, which does not even belong entirely to him".—*The Angel holding a candlestick* has always been judged more favourably than the other two. Mackowsky: "The angel shows the most individuality". But even here opinions differ. Jacob Burckhardt: "A charming little youthful head such as only Leonardo could have formed at that time". And Justi: "And then, naturally without clearly expressing his sarcastic intent, he makes an angel out of an ordinary workshop apprentice and the patron saint of the city out of a tramp". Michelangelo's angel is the male counterpart of the delicate female angel (about 1491–1494) by Niccolò dell' Arca, who executed the rest of the decoration of the shrine of St. Dominic;

Angel with Candlestick, by Niccolò dell' Arca, Bologna, San Petronio

Michelangelo's three figures are merely complements of Niccolò's work. Justi gave a concise opinion of them: "The three statuettes in Bologna—the fruits of a one year's stay in the city—are probably the most insignificant and least satisfactory works which have been handed down to us under Michelangelo's name, but it must be admitted that they are only too well authenticated". On the other hand, Henri Stendhal wrote: "These figures are most remarkable; we see quite clearly that this great artist began by imitating nature in the most painstaking way and that he knew how to render all her charm and morbidezza".—An *eagle* on the Palazzo Comunale in Bologna (Plate 123) is said to have been executed by Michelangelo during his first stay in Bologna in 1494; but almost everything about it contradicts this assumption.

Wölfflin, Jugendwerke, p. 17.—Frey, Leben, p. 203 f.; Quellen, p. 130 f.—Bode, Italienische Bildhauer, p. 168; Florentiner Bildhauer, p. 296.—Thode III, 88 f.; IV, 32 f.—Justi II, 46 f.—Aldo Foratti, Atti e memorie della R. Deputazione di Storia Patria per le provincie di Romagna, ser. IV, vol. VIII, fasc. IV–VI, 1918, p. 191 f.—Panofsky, col. 26–27.—F. Filippini, Michelangelo a Bologna, Bologna 1928.

CUPID. Plate 17 (18). Marble, 41¾ inches.—Not perfectly preserved; has been damaged by exposure to weather and by pistol-shots, especially about the belly; the right hand and head were broken off and stuck on again; the head probably not correctly replaced; the left arm (not visible in our photograph) was completed in modern times by Emilio Santarelli.[4] —Holroyd ("The work of a poor imitator"), Mackowsky and Kriegbaum, who attributes it to Vincenzo Danti (1530–1576), deny its authenticity; Berenson and Löwy, after hesitation, reject it.—Knapp dates it about 1498; Thode, about 1501; Wölfflin, about 1520.

Eric Maclagan, Michelangelo's Cupid, in Art Studies VI, Cambridge 1928, p. 3 f.—Michaelis, Z.f.b.K. XIII, 1878, p. 158 f.—Holroyd, p. 107 f.—Löwy, Kunstgeschichtliche Anzeigen 1913, p. 27 f.—Wölfflin, Jugendwerke, p. 30 f.—Symonds I, 62 f.—Justi II, 79 f.—Thode III, 118 f.—IV, 51 f.—Mackowsky, p. 392 f.—Frey, Leben, p. 319 f.— Grünwald, in Jahrb. d. allerh. Kaiserhauses, Vienna 1908 (XXVII).— F. Kriegbaum, in Jahrb. d. kunsthistorischen Samml. in Wien, new series, III, 1929, p. 247 f.

BACCHUS. Plate 19 (20–22; 122). Marble, 82 inches. According to Condivi's statement, executed for the Roman banker Jacopo Galli in his house. Commissioned in 1497, but perhaps not finished until 1499.[5] The Bacchus and Satyr are hewn out of one block.—Vasari was the first to notice the hermaphroditic element in the figure: "A marvellous blending of both sexes, uniting the slenderness of a youth with the fleshy roundness of a woman". To this Condivi adds: "The eyes are weak and lewd".—The pathological character of the figure has often repelled critics. Brinckmann calls it "the coarsest work by Michelangelo which we possess"; Mackowsky describes the "vice in a beaming youthful countenance" as an aesthetical error. Stendhal remarks: "Michelangelo divined the antique insofar as it expresses strength; yet the countenance is coarse and without charm". Similarly the poet Shelley wrote: "The countenance of this figure is the most revolting mistake of the spirit and meaning of Bacchus. It looks drunken, brutal, and

---

[4] The position of the legs is the same as in the "Venus Bathing" by Doidalsas of Bithynia, about 200 B.C. A free Renaissance imitation of this figure in bronze was made by Antico about 1495 (reproduced in Bode, Die italienischen Bronzestatuetten der Renaissance, Berlin 1922, plate 33). The whole question of the movement in the Cupid has never been satisfactorily explained; the expressive movements of Michelangelesque figures cannot be identified with definite processes. The nude on the left of Ezekiel in the Sistine Chapel ceiling and the St. Sebastian in the "Last Judgement" are similar in their expression of movement to the Cupid (*cf.* "Paintings", Plates 58 and 148).

[5] "The drunken Bacchus is, I believe, the figure which he began work on immediately after his arrival in Rome by order of Cardinal Riario and which he finished in a year; the Cardinal rejected it" (Johannes Wilde, in Mitteilungen d. kunsthist. Inst. in Florenz, Vol. IV, No. 1, p. 53 f.). With reference to a letter written by Michelangelo on July 2nd, 1496; "Whereupon the Cardinal asked me, whether I trusted myself to make something beautiful? I replied that I could not make such great things (as the antiques in his collection); but that he would see what I was able to do. We have now bought a piece of marble for a lifesize figure and I want to begin work on it next Monday (July 4th)".

narrow-minded, and has an expression of dissoluteness the most revolting ". He finds fault with the stiffness of the legs, quite wrongly, for they are a naturalistic expression of the semi-paralysed movements of the drunken god. All critics note the artistic perfection of the carving and the Christian element in this pagan theme. Michelangelo treated this subject again in a more clearly comprehensible manner ten years later in his " Drunkenness of Noah " in the frescoes of the Sistine Chapel. In both cases the sway of the sin of drunkenness is depicted, and in this first version, combined with beauty, it produces a tragically moving effect.

Frey, Leben, p. 285 f.—Thode III, 114 f.; IV, 46 f.—Symonds I, 58 f.—Justi II, 73 f.—Wölfflin, Jugendwerke, p. 26 f.—Mackowsky, p. 28 f.—Shelley (Forman's edition of the Prose Works), Vol. III, p. 71 f.—Stendhal, Histoire de la Peinture en Italie, 1817, chapter 136.

PIETÀ (Madonna della Febbre). Plate 23 (24–29). Marble, 69 inches.—The only work by Michelangelo with a genuine signature. The group was commissioned by Cardinal Jean de Villiers de la Grolaye (†1499), French Ambassador to the Holy See. The contract was made on August 26th, 1498, the price agreed upon being 450 ducats (the purchasing power of which in modern currency would be about £1,450).—The chief work of the youthful period, brilliantly described by Stendhal in his history of Italian painting, chapters 137–141.— The treatment of the subject was a complete novelty for Italy and many of Michelangelo's contemporaries considered it heretical; an orthodox writer of 1549 discovered a " Lutheran notion " in it. " The vesper painting was a theme which grew out of mysticism in Germany before 1300 and was also known in France in the fifteenth century. It is no mere chance that the commission for the first representation of this kind in Central Italy was given by a northerner " (Frida Schott-müller, note in her edition of Vasari). The idea of making the body of Christ smaller, so that it produces an effect of childlike helplessness in relation to the figure of the Madonna, is found in early German vesper sculptures. (Cf., for example, F. Lübbecke, Plastik des deutschen Mittelalters, Plate 72.) In Italy this treatment must have been known at the end of the fifteenth century from the paintings of Netherlandish artists such as Rogier van der Weyden and from miniatures in books of hours.[6]—Michelangelo's Pietà originally stood

in the Petronilla chapel, the so-called French chapel; after the demolition of this, about 1535, it was transferred to St. Peter's, at first to the Cappella della Febbre, or Fever Chapel; since 1749 it has been in the Cappella del Crocifisso.—In his " Cicerone " Jacob Burckhardt says : " The heads have a pure beauty which Michelangelo never achieved again in his later works ".

Thode III, 123 f.; IV, 56 f.—Justi II, 86 f.—Mackowsky, p. 31 f.— Wilhelm Pinder, Die Pietà, Leipzig 1922.

THE BRUGES MADONNA. Plates 31 (30, 32–36). Marble, 50 inches. The first mention of this work occurs in Albrecht Dürer's diary of his journey to the Netherlands, on April 7th, 1521 : "After this I saw the alabaster likeness of Mary in Our Lady, which Michelangelo made in Rome ". ("Alabaster" means white marble; "Our Lady", the church of Notre-Dame.)—Condivi, who never saw the work, which was brought to Bruges by Francesco del Pugliese in 1506, describes it as a round bronze image and says that the Bruges merchant Mouscron paid one hundred ducats for it.—Knapp (p. 176), following Wölfflin, dates it about 1504–1505.—The French sculptor David d'Angers claimed to have discerned the hand of an assistant.—The cast-down eyes of the Madonna suggested to Justi a comparison with Giorgione's Madonna in Castelfranco.—In Rembrandt's atelier there was a cast of the Child Jesus of the Bruges group. (In the 1656 inventory it is called " a child, by Michel Angelo ".) This cast of Rembrandt's is reproduced in a picture by Jan Lievens (Louvre, No. 129. Hans Schneider, Lievens, Haarlem 1932, Plate 14).

Thode III, 130 f.; IV, 59 f.—Justi II, 101 f.—Mackowsky, p. 53 f.

DAVID. (" The Giant ".). Plates 37, 41, 42 (38, 39, 40, 43). Marble, 216½ inches[7].—The contract was concluded on August 16th, 1501, with a term of delivery of two years and a fee which was eventually raised to 400 ducats. The statue was transported to the Piazza between the 14th and 18th May, 1503, and the consultation as to its erection took place on January 25th, 1504 (1505 according to the old Florentine calendar), Leonardo da Vinci and Botticelli being among those present. On September 8th, 1504, the erection in front of the Palazzo Vecchio in Florence was completed. In 1873 the statue was removed to the Accademia and in 1910 a marble replica was placed in front of the Palazzo Vecchio. Michelangelo was given a block of marble which Bartolomeo di Pietro had spoilt in Carrara and from which Agostino di Duccio had

---

[6] There is a clear relationship, not confined merely to the choice of subject, to the Pietà by Jacopo del Sellaio (1442–93), now in the Berlin Museum (Cat. No. 1055), especially as regards the pathetic opening of the Madonna's left hand, and the pendent right arm of the Christ. As this painting probably came from the church of San Frediano in Florence (Jahrb. d. preuss. Kunstsamml. XX, 1899, p. 195), it may very well have been familiar to Michelangelo. Similar points of resemblance may be detected elsewhere; the upright body of Christ in the Rondanini Pietà can be seen in Sellaio's Berlin Pietà (Cat. No. 111, 9 f.). According to Vasari, Jacopo del Sellaio was a pupil of Fra Filippo Lippi, whom Michelangelo, according to the same writer, frequently imitated.

[7] Schubring estimates its weight as about eighteen tons.

attempted to carve a David.—" So Michelangelo made a wax model of a youthful David holding the sling, which might serve as the ensigns of the Palace" (Vasari). When the Medici were driven out of Florence on April

David, crayon drawing by Leonardo da Vinci, about 1504, Windsor Castle

26th, 1527, the statue was damaged by a bench thrown out of one of the windows of the palace and the left arm was broken. The three pieces were found by Salviati and Vasari and replaced in 1543 by order of Duke Cosimo.— Jacob Burckhardt finds fault with the "pre-occupation with the model" seen in this statue and with the "mistake" of trying to represent the figure of an adolescent in colossal proportions. "Only grown persons can be conveniently enlarged. When seen through a diminishing glass, the David gains uncommonly in beauty and life ; to be sure with exception of the head, which seems to have been designed for quite a different mood." On the other hand, Justi writes : " His most perfect statue of a nude man, considered from a purely technical and plastic standpoint as life in marble ". Mackowsky notes the contrasts : " Constrained in its artistic elements, without enflaming the feelings. . . . Extremely austere and concise in its artistic expression ".

Gottschalk, Monatshefte für Kunstwissenschaft, I, 1908, p. 203 f.— Thode III, 175 f. ; IV, 75 f.—Justi II, 129 f.—Mackowsky, p. 42 f.— Frey, Jahrb. d. preuss. Kunsts. XXX, Supplement, p. 104 f.—Dvorak, II, 6 f.—Panofsky, col. 29.—Bode, Bertoldo, p. 97.

THE ROUND MADONNA RELIEF IN FLORENCE.

Plate 45 (44, 46). Marble, 32 inches.—Also known as the Pitti Madonna, after Bartolomeo Pitti who commissioned the work. Executed at approximately the same time as the other two round Madonnas, the " Madonna Taddei " in London (Plate 48) and the tempera painting, the " Madonna Doni ", in Florence (" Paintings ", Plate 6).—Justi notes the intimate character of the work and that it was intended " for the home " and not " for oratories or tombs ".—The relief used to be considered " unfinished ", but to modern eyes this does not appear to be the case.

Thode III, 155 f. ; IV, 115 f.—Mackowsky, 51 f.—Justi II, 184.— Symonds I, 111 f.

THE ROUND MADONNA RELIEF IN LONDON.

Plate 48 (47, 49). Marble, 42½ inches.—Also known as the Taddei Madonna, after its first owner, Taddeo Taddei.—Thode and Wölfflin think that the Pitti Madonna is the older of the two, Knapp and others, the Taddei tondo.—The relief is held to be unfinished and a number of opinions concerning its sketchiness have been collected by Justi (II, p. 190). Walter Pater wrote of it as follows :—" Michelangelo secures that ideality of expression which in Greek sculpture depends on a delicate system of abstraction, and in early Italian sculpture on lowness of relief, by an incompleteness, which is surely not always undesigned, and which, as I think, no one regrets, and trusts to the spectator to complete the half-emergent form ". The sculptor Guillaume thought that Michelangelo was following a special system to achieve an atmospherical loosening of the robust marble background, and compares it with " aerial perspective ", thus asserting his belief in a " painteresque element " in Michelangelo's sculpture. Michelangelo himself expressed his conception with aphoristic clarity in a letter to Benedetto Varchi (1549) : " Painting seems to me all the better, the nearer it approaches to relief, and relief to be all the worse the nearer it approaches to painting ". Within the framework of Michelangelo's works the two round reliefs represent his " small sculptures " and they should be compared with such ornamental works as Bertoldo's commemorative coins and Riccio's plaques. Justi notes " the genre-like " treatment of the Taddei Madonna, and the fact that it was " intended for a room in a bourgeois house ". He remarks : " A society painter of the eighteenth century might have appropriated this group without anybody noticing the lofty origin ". The subject : a child frightened by a fluttering bird which another child holds before him.

Justi II, 185 f. and 188 f.—Thode III, 158 f. ; IV, 115 f.—A. Grünwald, Florentiner Studien, Fig. 24.

ST. MATTHEW.

Plate 50 (51). Marble, 86⅝ inches. Unfinished.—Begun immediately after the David, the contract being concluded with the Florentine weavers' guild in April 1503, for twelve Apostles for the cathedral. In the winter of 1504–1505 Michelangelo was working mainly on his battle cartoon, in March 1505 he was summoned to Rome by Julius II, with whom he made a five-year contract for the tomb. After this, on December 18th, 1505, the contract for the Apostles was cancelled. When Michelangelo fled from Rome to Florence four months later, he appears to have resumed work on the St. Matthew (April to November 1506). At the end of November 1506 he joined the Pope in Bologna and began work on the large bronze portrait

(lost). The St. Matthew thus remained unfinished.—
Wölfflin and Justi think that most of the work on the
statue was done about 1504; Thode and Mackowsky,
about 1506. Mackowsky draws attention to a certain
influence of the Laocoön, discovered in 1506, especially

So-called "Pasquino", antique marble statue, Rome

in the expression and
poise of the head; Grün-
wald[8] that the antique
" Pasquino " was used
as a model. The treat-
ment of the draperies is
very similar to that of
the Ulysses statues (e.g.
Museo Chiaramonti, No.
704).—Attempts have
been made to create a
problem concerning the
St. Matthew; Dami
holds it to be a St.
Andrew and believes
that the sketched relief[9]
of a martyrdom of St.
Andrew in the Museo
Nazionale, Florence, is
the base belonging to it.

—But there have been some justified doubts concerning
it : Jacob Burckhardt in his " Cicerone " assumes a
later date of execution and a different purpose (" the
style obliges us to make such an assumption "), while
Justi says : " If the date of execution were not certain,
one would declare it to be a later work ". The connection
with the sculptures on the tomb of Julius executed ten
years later is apparent; the head of the St. Matthew
looks like an amplified sketch for the Moses, the whole
figure is closely akin to the " Captives " (*cf*. Plate 71),
which curiously enough have the same dimensions.—
"Although this statue—the embryo of a statue—is one
of the obscurest offshoots of his fantasy ", says Justi,
" it has always aroused keen interest, and even emotion
among artists and scholars ", and he adds : "As a
motive of statuary this St. Matthew is undoubtedly
strange and certainly contrary to all academic principles ".
He assumes that the technique was a " direct process ",
in other words, improvised carving from the block,
" omitting sketch and model ". He thinks that " chance "
led Michelangelo to a form of style which developed
into his last manner (*cf*. Plate 142, the body of Christ).
If the dating is correct, this important work marks the

beginning of a new period in Michelangelo's creative
career.[10]

Thode III, 198 *f.*; *IV*, 91 *f.*—*Justi II*, 202 *f.*—*Wölfflin, Jugendwerke*,
p. 56 *f.*—*Frey, Jahrbuch d. preuss. Kunsts. XXX*, 1909, *Supplement*,
p. 109 *f.*—*Mackowsky, p.* 76 *f.*—*L. Dami, in Dedalo VII*, 1926,
p. 29 *f.*—*Oscar Ollendorff, Rep. f. Kunstw.* 1898, *XXI, p.* 114.

THE TOMB OF POPE JULIUS. Plates 52–84;

124–128; 133–134.—First contract and first design,
March 1505. Forty statues and a payment of ten
thousand ducats over five years were agreed upon.
In April Michelangelo went to the quarries at Carrara;
in December he returned to Rome and set up a workshop in Piazza San Pietro. " If only my blocks of
marble would arrive from Carrara ! " he wrote to his
father on January 31st, 1506. " In this matter I think
I have the greatest ill-fortune. . . . A few days ago a
boat arrived which had all but been sunk owing to
contrary winds; and when I had succeeded in unloading
it, there came a flood and swamped everything in such
a way that I could not begin work ". The work thus
began without the blessing of the stars and elements.
Condivi called the story of its execution " The Tragedy
of the Tomb ".—On April 17th, 1506, Michelangelo
fled from Rome, feeling that he was not properly
appreciated by the Pope and that he had been grievously
offended. From Florence he wrote on May 2nd, 1506,
to Giuliano di San Gallo : " If I had stayed in Rome
any longer, it would have been a question not of the
Pope's tomb, but of my own. That was the reason of
my sudden departure ". But a few days later Roselli
wrote to Michelangelo that people were saying in Rome
that he was frightened by the idea of executing the
paintings in the Sistine Chapel. In Florence, Michelangelo perhaps resumed work on the battle cartoon;
the tomb seemed to have been forgotten. The Pope
had important political plans; he was thinking of war
and of reconquering for the Church her best territories.
On August 23rd, 1506, he left Rome and on November
11th he entered Bologna without encountering resistance.
He immediately summoned Michelangelo thither, in
order that he might cast his statue in bronze for the
reconquered city. " With the rope round his neck ",
as he himself expressed it, Michelangelo went to
Bologna; but the tomb seemed to have been forgotten

---

[8] A. Grünwald, Jahrb. d. kunsthist. Samml., Vol. XXVII, p. 130 f.

[9] Now attributed to Tribolo, formerly to Bandinelli; it is more likely to be
the work of Andrea Ferrucci da Fiesole.

[10] In his Life of Andrea Ferrucci da Fiesole Vasari says: "Andrea was
employed by the wardens of Santa Maria del Fiore to make the statue of an
Apostle, four braccia high (*about 7½ feet*). This was at the time when Cardinal
Giulio de' Medici was ruling in Florence (1519–1523): at the same time four
similar figures were allotted to four different masters: one to Benedetto da
Maiano, one to Jacopo Sansovino, a third to Baccio Bandinelli and a fourth
to Michelangelo Buonarroti ".—*According to this statement by Vasari, a new
date must be assigned to the St. Matthew, namely after* 1519. *This statue of an
Apostle would thus be contemporary with the four Boboli captives, which are of the same
height. The contract of* 1503 *with the Weavers' Guild cannot in that case refer to this
abbozzo. The drawings believed to be connected with the St. Matthew (Berenson* 1521,
1625 *and* 1399; *Frey* 5) *do, in fact, give the impression that they could hardly have
led to this result.* (Ferrucci's " St. Andrew " is usually dated 1512.)

again.—From 1508 to 1512 Michelangelo worked in Rome on the frescoes for the ceiling of the Sistine Chapel. After finishing them, he wanted to resume work on the tomb, but no agreement could be reached. In October 1512 he wrote to his father: " I am doing no work yet and am waiting for the Pope to tell me what I am to do ". On February 21st Julius II died and on May 6th a new contract was concluded with the executor of his will. Michelangelo undertook to execute the tomb in seven years and not to accept other work in the meantime ; he was to receive 1300 ducats in addition to the 3500 he had already had from Pope Julius. He submitted a revised design. Between 1513 and 1516 the *Moses* and the two *Captives* were executed (Plates 52, 60, 65). Michelangelo had a workshop at the Macello dei Corvi and employed Florentine stone-masons. In July 1516 a third contract was concluded and a reduced design was made, but there was a fresh interruption owing to the work on the designs for the façade of San Lorenzo. The following years were spent in unproductive work and in journeys to Florence and the marble quarries at Carrara, Pietrasanta and Seravezza. Only in 1519 was Michelangelo free again and he then worked on his statue of Christ and the " Boboli captives " for the tomb of Julius (Plates 68, 69, 72, 74) and on the " Victory ", which was probably intended for the same tomb (Plate 81). In 1520 the contract for the façade of San Lorenzo was definitely cancelled, but work on the Medici tombs was begun. In 1525, in the middle of the work on the Libreria Laurenziana, he first had the idea of completing the Julius monument as a wall-tomb. But no agreement was reached, although Michelangelo submitted a new drawing in October 1526, and he continued to work on the Medici tombs. The year 1529 was spent in work as an architect of fortifications. On April 29th, 1532, after long negotiations, a fourth contract was drawn up, but then came the execution of the " Last Judgement " and after its completion in 1542, the work on the tomb of Julius, which had long been in the hands of assistants, was entrusted entirely to Raffaello da Montelupo and Pietro Urbino. " I wish I had learnt in my youth to make matches ! " wrote Michelangelo in that year, " for then I should not be in such a state of agitation. . . . I do not want to go on living under this burden. . . . Only death or the Pope can release me from it. . . . I have wasted all my youth, chained to this tomb ".—The fifth contract (August 20th, 1542) laid down that Michelangelo was to execute only the Moses himself. In this last agreement everything was conceded that Michelangelo had asked for in his petition to Pope Paul III. " Master Michelangelo Buonarroti ", this document of July 20th, 1542, begins,

" undertook a long time ago to execute a tomb for Pope Julius. . . . "—" Master Michelangelo ", it says later, " shall be authorized to entrust three of the six statues destined for this tomb to a good and esteemed master . . . and the other three, among them the Moses, shall be by his own hand. But as Master Michelangelo gave the three statues named, which are already far advanced, namely the Madonna with the child on her arm in a standing posture, and a Prophet and a Sibyl, both seated, to the Florentine Raffaello da Montelupo . . . there remains for him only to complete with his own hand the three statues, namely Moses and the

The Tomb of Julius, lower story

two Captives, all three of which are almost finished. But as the two Captives mentioned were begun when the work was planned on a larger scale (a far larger number of statues had been contemplated, but in the contract of April 18th, 1532, the number was reduced), they are no longer suited to this project. . . . Wherefore Master Michelangelo began work on two other statues, which are to stand at the sides of Moses, namely the Contemplative and the Active Life,[11] which are fairly well advanced so that they can easily be completed by other masters ".—Michelangelo had then agreed to work for Pope Paul III " in his chapel ", that is to say in the Cappella Paolina, on the frescoes, a work which, in the sculptor's own words, " required a whole man freed from care ".—In February 1545 the monument was at last erected. " It can now be seen in San Pietro in Vincoli ",[12] wrote Condivi in 1553, " not as in the first design with four façades, but with *one* front, this being one of the smaller ones, not standing free, but against the wall. But although the work has been so patched up and reduced, it is the most worthy monument to be found in Rome and perhaps in the whole world,

---

[11] Plates 133, 134.

[12] Instead of in St. Peter's, as was originally planned.

on account of the three figures on it which are by the master's own hand ".

Justi I, 203–348.—Thode III, 243–294; IV, 127–230.—Mackowsky, p. 130 f.—Brinckmann, p. 44 f.—F. Burger, Das florentinische Grabmal bis Michelangelo, Strasbourg 1904, p. 313 f.—Karl Borinski, Die Rätsel Michelangelos : Michelangelo und Dante, Munich 1908, p. 111 f.—Dvorak II, p. 16 f.—Werner Weisbach, Trionfi, Berlin 1919.—Panofsky, col. 4, note ; col. 13, note ; col. 32.—On the Captives : Oscar Ollendorff, in Zeitschrift f. bild. Kunst, new series IX, 1897–98, and Repert. f. Kunstwissensch. XXI, 1898.—On the " Moses " : Robert Vischer, in Spemann's " Museum ", X, Leipzig 1905.

MOSES. On the tomb of Pope Julius. Plate 52 (53–58). Marble, 100½ inches. According to Thode (IV, 194), begun as early as 1506 ; according to Knapp (p. 178), the first consignment of marble from Carrara on June 24th, 1508,[13] was intended for the two Captives in the Louvre as well as for the Moses. Vasari says explicitly : " While Michelangelo was engaged on this work, the remainder of the marble blocks for the tomb arrived from Carrara and were unloaded at the Ripa ";—at that time the Pope had " his head full of Bologna matters " ; this must therefore have been in 1506.—Between the beginning of the work and its completion came the execution of the figures of Prophets on the ceiling of the Sistine Chapel, Joel and Jeremiah (1509–1510). The attitude of this statue is related to that of Giuliano de' Medici.—The Moses may be considered as an ideal portrait of Pope Julius II ; unfortunately we are no longer able to compare it with the colossal Bologna statue. " When Michelangelo had finished the Moses ", said Vasari in 1568, " there was no other work, whether ancient or modern, which could equal it ". He praises in particular the painteresque treatment of the hair, " one might almost believe that

St. John the Evangelist, marble statue by Donatello, about 1412–15, Florence, Cathedral

the chisel had become a brush ". Stendhal in 1817 said : " Those who have not seen this statue, cannot realize the full power of sculpture ". But he also mentions the " profound disparagement " which had been the statue's lot and quotes the sculptor Falconnet, who declared that the Moses was more like a galley-slave than a divinely inspired lawgiver, and the painter Fuseli, who discovered in it a resemblance to a satyr or a "goat's face".[14] About this time Goethe laid great store by a small bronze copy of the Moses.—A hundred years ago, the painter Haydon wrote in the Encyclopædia Britannica of the " bullying defiance of Moses ". The sculptor David d'Angers also spoke of a " barbarian chief ", and Jacob Burckhardt gives it only summary praise and finds fault with many of its details : " But the head is unsatisfactory both as to the shape of the skull and as to physiognomy, while as to the magnificently treated beard . . . far too much fuss is made ; the celebrated left arm has, in reality, nothing to do except press this beard to the body ".—It is not the appreciation of Renaissance art but a comprehension of Baroque which enables us to see the Moses in a proper light ; it is a question whether the younger generation is not losing

---

[13] Michelangelo's accompanying letter mentions " the large statue ", " two statues " and " the statue of His Holiness ". There were thus four figures hewn in the rough.

[14] Histoire de la Peinture en Italie, par M. Beyle, chapters 160 and 165.

1. *Pope Julius II, silver-point drawing by Michelangelo, about 1508, Florence, Uffizi.*—2. *Zacharias, ceiling of the Sistine Chapel about 1509.*—3. *Moses, about 1513–16*

its ability to see again.[15] This is a particularly striking example of the transitory nature of all artistic criteria and shows how apparently similar opinions from different periods are based on different spheres of experience. Psycho-analysis has attempted to approach the Moses in its own way (Imago III, 1914, p. 15 f.). —The costume is imitated from antique statues of barbarians (an attempt at historical accuracy), the horns represent rays of light. "The rest is entirely in the antique style", says Condivi.—Michelangelo's Moses has often been compared with Donatello's St. John the Evangelist, for instance by Lord Balcarres (Donatello, London, 1903, p. 16): "In the Moses, with all its exaggeration and melodrama, with its aspect of frigid sensationalism, which led Thackeray to say he would not like to be left alone in the room with it, we find every motionless limb imbued with vitality and the essentials of movement. The Moses undoubtedly springs from the St. John, transcending it as Beethoven surpassed Haydn. In spite of nearly unpardonable faults verging on decadence, it is the greater though the less pleasing creation of the two. The St. John surveys the world; the Moses speaks with God".

THE DYING AND THE HEROIC CAPTIVES.
Intended for the tomb of Pope Julius. Plates 60 and 65 (59, 61–64, 66, 67). Marble, 90½ and 86½ inches.— These two statues were not used for the tomb because, as we learn from Michelangelo himself, they could not be fitted into the reduced design. In 1544, when the tomb was erected, the master was lying ill in the palace of Roberto Strozzi. The latter, a cousin of Caterina de' Medici and great-grandson of Lorenzo il Magnifico, the owner of banking houses in Rome and Lyons, with influence at the French Court, conspired against Duke Cosimo de' Medici and shared with Michelangelo the ambition of restoring Florence to its republican freedom. Michelangelo presented the two statues to him in 1544 and six years later Strozzi gave them to King Henri II of France, who presented them to the Constable Anne de Montmorency for his castle of Écouen; in 1632 they were the property of Cardinal Richelieu; in the eighteenth century they became state property and so passed to the Louvre. The antique models for these Captives were not the statues of fettered barbarians, but the Hellenistic representations of Marsyas, which survived in mediæval figures of St. Sebastian.

—Ever since Condivi's time, captious attempts have been made to discover the allegorical significance of the "Captives"; almost every possible suggestion has been made, down to "the personification of the mass for the dead".—Condivi writes: "Between the niches there should have been hermes-columns, to which, on cube-shaped projections, other statues were bound like captives. These represented the liberal arts and in the same manner painting, sculpture and architecture, each statue with its attributes, making them easily recognizable. This was supposed to mean that all the fine arts had died at the same time as Pope Julius".—Oscar Ollendorff has interpreted the Captives in the platonic sense (Michelangelos Gefangene im Louvre, Z.f.b.K., new series IX, 1897–98), Werner Weisbach as triumphal symbols (Trionfi, Berlin 1919, p. 109 f.). Vasari gave them a political interpretation which has not since been maintained: "These Captives represent the provinces which the Pope subjugated and incorporated in the Papal States".—If we ignore all these conjectures and also those of Justi, Thode, Brockhaus and Borinski, if we wish to see nothing except that which the works themselves clearly reveal to us as soon as we approach them with our eyes and our perceptions, then these Captives become easily comprehensible, eternally human symbols: captives of life, of dreams and of death, struggling against the bonds of fate and relentless Nature, Titans who wrestle in vain or who glide into redeeming unconsciousness. In this sense these eternally vanquished beings become the counterparts of the temporal conquerors, the Victories.

Marsyas, copper engraving after an antique statue in Rome, from Montfaucon's "Antiquitates" (1719-22)   *Michelangelo, wax model for a Captive (cf. Plate 75), London, Victoria and Albert Museum*

[15] G. K. Chesterton ("The Resurrection of Rome", London 1934, p. 42 and 45) remarked irreverently: "I know all that there is to be said against the rococo quality of the Renaissance. It did marvels in statuary, or sculpture in the round; but many may feel that the statues are rather too round. . . . The Pontiffs were great patrons of sculpture. One of them is responsible for raising, or trying to raise, that incredible army of statues, which was to occupy the city like a multitudinous invasion of the gods; and of which one or two remain, not altogether unnoticed, like monsters after a flood; such as that strange horned and bearded god or monster, to whom his great maker gave the name of Moses".

THE FOUR UNFINISHED CAPTIVES. Intended for the tomb of Pope Julius. Plates 68, 69, 73, 75 (70, 71, 72, 74, 76, 77, 78). Marble, 90½ inches.— Inserted by Duke Cosimo I de' Medici, who received them from Michelangelo's nephew, into artificial stalactites in a grotto at the entrance to the Boboli gardens in Florence; later transferred to the Accademia. —Mackowsky has made a technical study of these figures (p. 148 f.), for they are "more suitable than almost any other work of the master's for deducing valuable conclusions as to Michelangelo's methods". He declares that Michelangelo did not transform a finished model into marble following the schematic method of point-setting, but that he hewed into the block from one side in the manner of relief. Justi arrived at the same conclusion, quoting the descriptions of Michelangelo's methods by Vasari and Cellini and likewise referring to the unfinished statues, the St. Matthew and the four Captives in the Boboli gardens. Justi speaks of an "extraction of the statue out of the block from the front" (Justi I, 358 f.). "Anyone who knew nothing of its genesis, would think that the St. Matthew was an unfinished relief. Here we have the front half of a figure, the parts seen in profile or frontally having been carried to different degrees of completion; the other, rear portion is still hidden in the untouched, square block. . . . But this apparent half-relief was intended to become a statue in the round".—Mackowsky speaks of the tools used: "Nowhere can we find traces of the auger;[16] the whole of the work was done with pointing-irons and dented chisels. In consequence the surface shows parallel strokes which remind us of hatching".—Michelangelo's "sculptural handwriting" which has otherwise been studied only in connection with the Boboli slaves, has been examined by Alois Grünwald (Florentiner Studien, Dresden 1914) in relationship to the later works.

THE VICTORY. Probably intended for the tomb of Pope Julius. Plate 82 (79–81, 83, 84). Marble, 102 inches.—Knapp (p. 179) surmises that the group was executed after 1520 and intended for the façade of San Lorenzo; Brinckmann (p. 85 f.) likewise opines that it was not intended for the tomb of Julius and believes it to be an allegory of the platonic Eros. On the other hand F. Schottmüller (note to her edition of Vasari VII, 2, p. 319) and Panofsky (col. 13) are against this theory. Justi (II, 285 f.) interprets it politically as an allegory on the overthrow of freedom

in Florence;[17] he describes the group as "probably the most puzzling work which Michelangelo has bequeathed to posterity".—Mackowsky (p. 151) suspects the collaboration of assistants on account of the "exaggerated modelling", and dates it about the same time as the Apollo, which was executed after 1530, thus assigning it to the same period as Justi. There is firm support for the dating in the fact that Seravezza marble was used, the quarries there having been opened in 1518.—A resemblance between the features of the "Vanquished"[18] and those of Michelangelo (Plates 79 and 138) was noted by the older writers (Symonds I, 89); on the assumption that the young Cavaliere, Michelangelo's friend, was the model for the Victor, it was easy to arrive at an erotic interpretation: Destruction through Love. This would then be a counterpart to the later self-portrait of Caravaggio as the head of Goliath in the hands of David, or, in a different manner, to the self-portrait of Cristofano Allori as the head of Holofernes in front of the beautiful Judith.

THE RISEN CHRIST (Cristo Risorto). Plates 85, 86 (87, 88). Marble, 82 inches.—The apron, shoe and halo are later additions; half of the apron has now been removed. — Commissioned on June 15th, 1514, by Metello Vari and two other Romans, in return for a fee of 200 ducats. A black vein was found in the marble, disfiguring the face, and Michelangelo had to begin the work again. This first version, since lost, was seen by Aldovrandi in 1556 at the house of Vari. Owing to this defect in the marble the work was interrupted in 1516; the new block from Carrara had not arrived by December 21st, 1518.[19] On that date Michelangelo

The Risen Christ, photographed without the Baroque additions

[16] The auger was used by Michelangelo in his early period, particularly in the "Drunken Bacchus".

[17] Justi is here referring to the siege and capture of Florence by the Medici in 1530, when Michelangelo supervised the defence-works (not to the victory of the Medici in 1512).

[18] There is a late echo of this Victory group in the "Apotheosis of Prince Eugen" by Balthasar Permoser, 1721, in which the "Vanquished" is actually an authentic self-portrait of the artist (reproduced in Ludwig Goldscheider, 500 Self-portraits, London 1936, Plate 295). In the Bargello at Florence there are two imitative repetitions of Michelangelo's Victory composition, one by Vincenzo Danti, and the other, with a female figure, by Giambologna. Vincenzo de' Rossi's "Samson slaying a Philistine" in Palazzo Vecchio is likewise an imitation of Michelangelo's Victory group.

[19] It is possible, however, that the statement in the letter of 1518 is an excuse, and that the block four braccia high (92 inches) which Michelangelo purchased on April 25th, 1517, was intended for the Christ (Ricordi 568).

wrote to Lionardo Sellaio in Rome. " I am also being pressed by Signor Metello Vari about his statue, which is in Pisa[20] and should come on one of the first boats. I have never answered him and shall not write to you any more until I have begun the work ; for I am dying of grief and against my will appear to myself as a swindler ". The barges bringing the marble from Carrara had been held up in Pisa owing to the drying-up of the Arno. In the same letter Michelangelo speaks of his new atelier in Florence, on the Piazza Ognissanti, which he had set up for the execution of his sculptures for San Lorenzo. The second version of the Christ was created in this atelier between the beginning of 1519 and April 1520. Michelangelo's assistant Pietro Urbino was sent to Rome to erect the statue in Santa Maria sopra Minerva and to finish it there. But on September 6th, 1520, Sebastiano del Piombo wrote in a letter to Michelangelo : " I must tell you that Pietro Urbino has ruined everything that he has worked upon. Especially the toes of the right, completely visible foot, which he has hewn off entirely, also he has shortened the fingers of the hands, especially those of the right hand holding the Cross, so that Frizzi says they look as if they had been made by a baker of cracknels. . . . Also one can see clearly what he has been up to with the beard, any apprentice could have done it more cleverly. . . . Then, too, he has knocked one of the nostrils about—a little more and God alone could have put this nose right ! . . . Pietro thinks he is a great master—poor man, he will never learn what it means to make such figures—for the knees of this statue are worth more than the whole of Rome ". Federigo Frizzi repaired and completed the statue. Despite this Michelangelo proposed to his customer Vari that he should make a new statue, that is to say a third version, for he would hardly have made a replica. But Vari, who had waited seven years for this work, wanted no improvements : " It shows the loftiness of your mind, that you wish to replace a work which could not be better by another that is better ". On September 27th, 1521, the statue was unveiled ; on January 12th Sebastiano del Piombo wrote to Michelangelo : " The statue makes a very good impression. All the same I have said and caused to be said, in all places where it seemed to me fitting, that the execution is not by your hand ". It is certain that many of the displeasing elements in this statue, such as its excessive smoothness and the too ornamental treatment of the hair and beard, must be ascribed to the assistant.—The painter Benjamin Haydon found fault with the anatomy : " The figure of Michelangelo's Christ standing with

a cross, has the spine of the scapula prominent and bony, and all muscles shrinking from it, the characteristics of a thin man ; whilst the spine of the ilium of the same figure in front, is entirely covered by the muscles around it, the marks of a muscular and fleshy man ". Michelangelo's idea of Christ as shown in this work is in accordance with the Renaissance, the triumphant Saviour, the apotheosis of the hero ; not the Gothic conception of the Son of Man, suffering and vanquished by death.—Herman Grimm was reminded of an Achilles.

The Medici Chapel, Florence, San Lorenzo, Sagrestia Nuova

THE FUNERARY CHAPEL FOR THE MEDICI FAMILY. Plates 94, 95 ; 90 ; 124 ; 126 (89, 91, 92, 93, 96–121, 145 ; 125, 127, 128.)—Commissioned by Cardinal Giulio de' Medici, afterwards Pope Clement VII. Originally, in 1520, planned as a separate edifice with four tombs, for Lorenzo il Magnifico, Giuliano the Elder, Giuliano Duke of Nemours (†1516), son of Lorenzo il Magnifico, and Lorenzo Duke of Urbino (†1519), grandson of Lorenzo il Magnifico ; then as mural decoration with two sarcophagi on each wall ; then with the addition of a double tomb for the two Medici Popes, Leo X and Clement VII ; executed after 1524 in its final form, which underwent various modifications during the work. The figure of the Madonna (Plate 90), which had been projected from the first, was to have been placed on the papal tomb. The final solution was that the papal tomb and those for the Magnifici were omitted, and the project was limited to two separate tombs for the Dukes.—On the various modifications of the project an exhaustive study has been made by A. E. Popp (Die Medicikapelle Michelangelos, Munich 1922) ; there is a chronological table of all the works in Brinckmann, p. 57–59.—The construction of the chapel was begun in March 1521 and the cupola was in position by January 1524. The *Madonna* was begun in 1525, should have been finished by the winter of 1531–32, but was still unfinished in

---

[20] He means, of course : hewn in the rough.

the autumn of 1534 when Michelangelo moved to Rome to paint the " Last Judgement " in the Sistine Chapel.— Of the four recumbent figures the *Aurora* was begun first (Plate 103) ; the dates of execution being : *Aurora* 1521–1531 ; *Crepusculo* (Plate 102), 1524–1531 ; *Notte* (Plate 100), 1525–1531 ; *Giorno* (Plate 101), 1525–1534, unfinished.—Statue of *Lorenzo* (Plate 96), 1524–1534 ;

Roman Marble Torso, Rome, Museo Mussolini　　*Detail from Michelangelo's " Crepusculo ", San Lorenzo*

statue of *Giuliano* (Plate 97), 1531–1534.—In addition to these, four river-gods were planned, which were to have lain by the sarcophagi ; models for them in clay and bronze by Ammanati after Michelangelo, were found in Florence (A. Gottschewski, in Münchener Jahrbuch I, 1906, p. 43 f.).—Work of assistants : Tribolo began the " Earth " for the tomb of Lorenzo ; neither the model nor the abbozzo of the statue has been preserved ; Montelupo carved, after Michelangelo's

Fra Giovanni Montorsoli (after Michelangelo), St. Cosmas, Florence, San Lorenzo　*Raffaello da Montelupo (after Michelangelo), St. Damian, Florence, San Lorenzo*

model, the " Damian " on the left of the Madonna ; Montorsoli, who assisted in the completion of the " Giuliano ", made by himself the " Cosmas " on the other side of the Madonna.—" The crouching boy " (Plate 124) was probably intended, together with three similar unexecuted pieces, to crown the entablature (Popp, Medicikapelle, p. 142) ; the "Apollo" (Plate 126) is likewise said to have been designed as a niche

figure for the Medici Chapel (Popp, p. 172).—Various attempts have been made to interpret the allegorical meaning of the monument : Borinski saw in it references to Dante ; Steinmann, to a carnival song ; Brockhaus, to Ambrosian hymns ; all three of them thus derive it from literature.—Jacob Burckhardt's opinion of the chapel (1855) was as follows : "Architecture and sculpture are conceived together in such a way, as if the master had previously modelled both out of one and the same clay ". On the other hand the French painter Henri Regnault declared (1867) : " I made a pilgrimage to the Medici Chapel. What wonderful blocks of marble live and move there ! Unfortunately they are in a bad setting. This architecture, which is ascribed to Michelangelo, made me quite mad. It is common and without charm, and it reduces and destroys the figures. These little mausoleums, these tiny pillars and windows which surround the divine figures of the Thinker and of Giuliano, made me turn pale with anger ".

Karl Frey, Studien zu Michelangelo, Jahrb. d. preuss. Kunstsamml., 1896.—G. Gronau, Jahrbuch XXXII, Supplement, p. 62–81.— A. Grünwald, Jahrb. d. allerh. Kaiserhauses 1907.—Thode I, 291–315 ; III, 413–463 ; IV, 431–544.—Justi II, 213–274.—Panofsky, col. 14, 15.—A. E. Popp, Die Medicikapelle Michelangelos, Munich 1922.— Gerald S. Davies, Life of Michelangelo, London 1909, p. 141.—Fritz Burger, Geschichte des florentinischen Grabmals, Strasbourg 1904.— Wilhelm Köhler, Neuere Literatur über die Entstehungsgeschichte von Michelangelos Medici-Kapelle, Kunstgeschichtl. Anzeigen IV, 1907.— Ernst Steinmann, Das Geheimnis der Medicigräber, Leipzig 1907.— Karl Borinski, Die Rätsel Michelangelos, Munich 1908.—Heinrich Brockhaus, Michelangelo und die Medicikapelle, Leipzig 1911.—Deutsche Rundschau 1890 (articles by E. Brücke and W. Henke on the "Aurora" and " Night ").—Oscar Ollendorff, Über Michelangelos allegorische Gestalten in der Mediceischen Kapelle, Preuss. Jahrbücher, vol. 81, 1895, and Zeitschrift f. bild. Kunst, new series XX, 1909.—On the same subject : Georg Warnecke, Kunst-Chronik, new series, vol. V, 1893–94.— Maximilian von Groote, Die Deutung der Medici-Grabmäler ("Zur Kunstgeschichte des Auslandes", Strassburg, 1900 f., vol, 122).

MADONNA AND CHILD. Belongs to the Medici tombs. Plate 90 (89, 91, 92). Marble, $81\frac{1}{2}$ inches.— There is no parallel to this statue in Renaissance sculpture ; on the other hand it is in every way akin to Roman Imperial art, for example the " Juno suckling the infant Hercules ", Museo Chiaramonti, No. 241.— Jacob Burckhardt in his " Cicerone " says of Michelangelo's Madonna : " It is hardly more than hewn from the rough. . . . Owing to a defect in the marble or a slip on the part of the artist, the left arm did not turn out as it should have done and it was then adjusted behind as we see it to-day. Probably this affected the rest of the statue, which for that reason was completed only schematically and inadequately ".—Such was the incomprehension of the preceding century for Michelangelo, despite its flow of words. Carl Justi remarked thereon : " We live in an age of ' revision of all values ', of a fundamental transformation of the world of culture ; and thus it happens that the most criticized of Michelangelo's marble figures, which previously was almost ignored, is now the most praised, as the most powerful expression of his style ".

LORENZO DE' MEDICI. Belonging to the Medici tombs. Plate 96 (99). Marble, 71 inches. — Known as the " Pensieroso ", the Thinker. Vasari speaks of "il pensoso duca ", the thoughtful duke. — The attitude has precedents in Roman antique statues of philosophers. (It is irrelevant whether Michelangelo may have known this or that antique statue, for Roman sculpture was based on the repetition of types ; on the other hand Etruscan or antique Roman artistic traits in Michelangelo's works may be attributed to hereditary tendencies.)

Antique statue of a Philosopher, Rome, Museo Capitolino

GIULIANO DE' MEDICI. Belonging to the Medici tombs. Marble, 71 inches. Plate 97 (93, 98).— Steinmann (Das Geheimnis der Medicigräber, fig. 27, 28) believes in an inspiration from Byzantine reliefs of " holy warriors " on the façade of St. Mark's, Venice. In his opinion the details on the coat of mail were executed by an assistant.—The poet Samuel Rogers owned a wax model, " looking ominous " (Jameson, Memoirs of Early Italian Painters, new edition, London 1859, p. 199). There is another copy, and also wax models of the Giuliano[21] and the Madonna, in the National Gallery, Edinburgh.—In the statues of the two Dukes Michelangelo made no effort to achieve fidelity of portraiture ; to the Florentines, who missed this lifelikeness and who were puzzled by the purely artistic conception, Michelangelo replied proudly that in a thousand years' time nobody would know what the two Medicis really looked like.

THE FOUR PHASES OF THE DAY. Medici tombs. Plates 100-103 (104-121 ; 145).—Stendhal says : " The statues in San Lorenzo are partly unfinished. This deficiency is rather an advantage in view of Michelangelo's powerful style ". Stendhal was also the first to draw attention to the resemblances to the Vatican " Torso " (Catalogue, No. 3).[22] " In the two male figures ", he says (Histoire de la Peinture en Italie, chapter 158), " of ' Day ' and ' Dusk ', one finds striking reminiscences of the Vatican torso, but transformed by Michelangelo's genius ". Burckhardt, in his " Cicerone ", writes : " In these four statues the master has proclaimed his boldest ideas on the aim and limits of his art. . . . For his successors this was the straight road to ruin ". Vasari wrote : "And what can I say of the Night, this statue which is not only a great and rare work of art, but is also unique ? Who, in any period, has ever seen a statue, whether ancient or modern, of such high culture ? One can understand that it was this Night which completely obscured all those artists who for a time sought, not to surpass, but to equal Michelangelo ". —Daniele da Volterra copied all the figures in the Medici Chapel, and Tintoretto and El Greco, among others, worked from these copies.

Hercules, antique statue in the former Maffei Collection, Rome, copper engraving after Montfaucon   *Recumbent figure from an urn, Etruscan about 500 B.C., Florence, Museo Archeologico*

THE CROUCHING BOY. Belonging to the Medici tombs. Plate 124 (125). Marble, 22 inches.—Unfinished. Its authenticity is unproved, and doubtful.—Compare Plate 5.—C. Frey dates it 1497, before the Bacchus.— Hewn out of a square block, with maximum utilization of the volume.—This figure, conceived as a crowning of the entablature, reminds us with its economy of height

---

[21] Plate VI.—Knapp, Klassiker der Kunst, p. 106, reproduces the models of the two dukes, but states erroneously that they were in Florence. Thode (VI, p. 278) erroneously assumed that the model of the Lorenzo came from the Rogers collection ; actually it came from the Campbell collection and was found at Siena in 1844, while the other copy was seen by Passavant (Kunstreise, 1833, p. 87) in Rogers' collection at a much earlier date.

[22] Discovered at the time of Pope Julius II.—Albertino, writing in 1510, mentions the following antiques among others : the Horse-tamers of Monte Cavallo, the Belvedere Apollo, Hercules with the child Bacchus, Commodus as Hercules, the wolf of the Capitol, the equestrian statue of Marcus Aurelius. The Laocoön was found in 1506 and is said to have been restored in accordance with Michelangelo's suggestions. The following three antique sculptures seem to have exercised most influence on the four statues in the Medici Chapel : Ariadne (found in 1512), the Nile (found in 1513) and the other river-god, the so-called Marforio (now in the courtyard of the Museo del Campidoglio Catalogue, No. 1), which was discovered in the Middle Ages and at the time of the Renaissance was very popular, like the " Pasquino ". The formation of Michelangelo's recumbent figures, however, was an inheritance from the figures on Etruscan sarcophagi ; details, such as the mask of Night, can be found in a similar form on various statues from the Roman Imperial period. (Thode V, 301, on the river-god with urn and mask in the Vatican, and other antique works.)

of the figures on the gable-corners of antique temples. It has not much in common with the " Boy removing

Girl bathing, small Florentine bronze about 1520, London, British Museum

a thorn from his foot ", but more with the so-called " Grinder " (Florence), which was found before 1538.

Thode V, 284.—Carl Frey, Allgemeine Zeitung, No. 276, 277.— Mackowsky, p. 196.

APOLLO (or David ?). Plate 126 (127, 128). Marble, 58¾ inches.—In 1527 the Medici were driven out for the second time ; but the Emperor Charles V joined forces with Pope Clement VII and laid siege to Florence (Michelangelo at this time was responsible for the fortifications) ; the city fell after eleven months (August 12th, 1530) and Alessandro de' Medici, probably an illegitimate son of Clement VII and husband of Margaret, later Duchess of Parma, the illegitimate daughter of Charles V, was installed as hereditary duke. Vasari tells us : "After the capitulation of Florence, Baccio Valori, as the Pope's representative, was ordered to arrest some of the chief party-leaders from among the burghers. The court sent to Michelangelo's house to seek him, but his suspicions had been aroused and he fled to the house of a friend near-by ". The Pope ordered that he should be found and promised him immunity from punishment if he would continue his work on the Medici Chapel. " When Michelangelo felt himself thus reassured, he sought first to win the favour of Baccio

Valori. He made for him from a block of marble, three braccia high, a figure which represents Apollo drawing an arrow from his quiver. This statue, which was not quite finished, now stands in the chamber of the Prince of Florence ".—A. E. Popp (Die Medicikapelle, p. 172) describes this statue as a niche figure for the tomb of Lorenzo and does not believe that it is the statue intended for Valori, maintaining that the latter is the apocryphal bronze Apollo in the Louvre discovered by Jan Six (Gazette des Beaux-Arts, LXIII, 1921, 166 f. ; *cf.* Panofsky, col. 57). It is permissible to assume that the statue when it was begun was destined for the Medici Chapel, but that Michelangelo then gave it away to Baccio Valori, just as he gave the rejected figures from the other tomb to Strozzi. Vasari's statements correspond exactly with this statue, both as regards measurements and material and dating. The elevation beneath the foot is, in my opinion, not the head of Goliath, but an undulation in the ground or a stone.

Thode V, 185.—Cosimo Conti, La prima Reggia di Cosimo, Florence 1893, I, 35.—Mackowsky, p. 151.

BRUTUS. Plate 129 (130–132). Marble, 25½ inches.— On the pedestal is inscribed the distich : Dum Bruti effigiem sculptor de marmore ducit, In mentem sceleris venit et abstinuit. (While he was hewing the effigy of Brutus out of the marble, he came upon the spirit of crime and the artist stopped.) According to tradition this inscription was composed by the Venetian humanist Pietro Bembo (1470–1547). On the other hand the Anonimo Morelliano states that Bembo had an antique marble head of Brutus in his house at Padua ; this bust, according to the Anonimo, represented an orator ; curiously enough, Guillaume also said of Michelangelo's Brutus that it gave the effect of a passionate orator (Thode V, 288). We may assume that Michelangelo knew this Brutus, and that either he saw it when he was in Venice in 1529 or that Bembo, after being made a cardinal in 1539, brought it with him when he moved to Rome. In 1568 Vasari maintained that the actual inspiration came from Donato Giannotti and that the work was commissioned by Cardinal Ridolfi. In his Dialogues written in 1545, Giannotti makes Michelangelo speak of Brutus :[23] " He who murders a tyrant, does not kill a man, but a beast in human form. For as all tyrants are devoid of that love which all men by nature must have for their neighbours, so too they are without human feelings and therefore not men, but beasts. That tyrants have no love for their neighbours, is obvious, for otherwise they would not have taken what

---

[23] It is not certain whether this is an elaboration of words actually spoken by Michelangelo ; the passage may be fictitious, inspired perhaps by Michelangelo's bust of Brutus.

belongs to others and they would not have become tyrants by oppressing others. I speak naturally of usurpers and not of hereditary princes who govern their states by the will of the people."—According to Vasari, Michelangelo entrusted the bust of Brutus to Tiberio Calcagni in order that he might finish it : " He himself had executed only the features of the Brutus with fine strokes of the graduating iron." On this point Carl Justi wrote (II, 301) : " The head of Brutus remained at the stage of a sketch ; only the draperies were elaborated ; this trite and insignificant work is neither by the hand nor in the style of the master ". A. Grünwald (Florentiner Studien, p. 11) has investigated Calcagni's share in the work ; the retouching concerns mainly the robe and the neck, but in addition to this the chin and mouth and a part of the hair have been gone over roughly with a coarsely crenated flat-iron, an instrument which was never used by Michelangelo. —The resemblance to busts of Roman emperors has frequently been noted. This resemblance, however, is due to the toga and the shape of the bust, which were Calcagni's work. If we are to credit Vasari's statement, Michelangelo left the block untouched at this point, and the bust would produce a more imposing effect if it had been left like that.—Fritz Knapp (p. 181) remains faithful to the old political interpretation and thinks that the bust is a reminder of the murder of Alessandro de' Medici by Lorenzino.

Thode III, 476 f. ; V, 287 f.—Justi II, 298 f.—Symonds II., 252 f.— Mackowsky, 236 f.—Alois Grünwald, Florentiner Studien, Dresden 1914 (1920).—F. Portheim, Rep. f. Kunstw. 1889, XII, p. 151 f.— Panofsky, col. 25.

THE ACTIVE AND THE CONTEMPLATIVE LIFE.

On the tomb of Pope Julius (cf. the note on Plates 52–84). Marble, 80 and 81½ inches. Plates 133, 134.—Mainly by Michelangelo's hand, but finished and polished by assistants (A. Grünwald, Florentiner Studien, p. 16 f.). On July 20th, 1542, Michelangelo proposed that these figures, which he had already begun, should be substituted for the Captives, as the latter no longer fitted the niches. According to Vasari, Michelangelo executed the statues in " less than a year " ; they must therefore have been finished in 1543.—Vasari also says that the figure symbolizing Active Life is Leah, while that symbolizing Contemplative Life is Rachel. Leah is not holding a mirror in her right hand, but a diadem, through which she has already drawn the tresses of her hair. Condivi does not speak of Rachel and Leah, but calls the statues simply Active and Contemplative Life.[24] He also says : " In these

[24] Michelangelo himself, in his memorandum of July 20th, 1542, to Pope Paul III, likewise calls them Active and Contemplative Life, and not Leah and Rachel.

works Michelangelo, always a zealous student of Dante, has followed the poet, to whom in his Purgatorio the Countess Matilda appears as personification of active life in a flowery meadow ". The Margravine Matilda of Tuscany, who was a witness of Emperor Henry IV's humiliation at Canossa (1077) and left all her possessions to the Roman Church, was believed by Michelangelo (Condivi, Chapter 1) to be one of his ancestresses, and the "Active Life " would thus be her monument. The passages from Dante which Vasari[25] and Condivi mention as referring to Rachel and Leah and to Matilda and Beatrice are the following :

> " If any ask my name, then let him know
> That I am Leah, and I move alway
> Fair hands to wreathe myself a garland so.
> Here at my glass I joy in my array ;
> But never does my sister Rachel rise
> Up from her mirror where she sits all day ".
> (*Purgatorio*, xxvii, 100–105.)

The meeting with Matilda, the guardian of Paradise, occurs in Canto xxviii, line 118 f., where she appears with Beatrice.—In this respect, therefore, Condivi's statement differs from Vasari's, and this has been the cause of considerable confusion.

Thode I, 437 ; III, 288 f. ; IV, 140, 220 f.—Mackowsky, p. 152 f.— Justi I, 336 f.

THE FLORENCE PIETÀ (Entombment).

Plate 137 (135, 136, 138–140). Marble, 92 inches.—Mentioned by Vasari in his first edition (1550) and must thus have been begun before 1550. In the same year the French traveller Blaise de Vigenère saw Michelangelo working on it : " I saw Michelangelo at work. He had passed his sixtieth year, and although he was not very strong, yet in a quarter of an hour he caused more splinters to fall from a very hard block of marble than three young masons in twice or thrice the time. No one can believe it who has not seen it with his own eyes. And he attacked the work with such energy and fire that I thought it would fly into pieces. With one blow he

[25] It should be noted that Vasari does not explicitly mention Dante. Michelangelo must have known the allegory of Active and Contemplative Life from the " Disputationes Camaldulenses, the Conversations in the Convent of Camaldoli by Cristoforo Landino. Landino was a member of the neoplatonic circle around Lorenzo de' Medici, and his Disputationes Camaldulenses were written about 1470. (Manuscript by Pietro Cennini, 1476, in the Biblioteca Laurenziana at Florence.—Bandini, Specimen litt., vol. II, pp. 188 f.—First known impression : Strasbourg 1508.—The Disputationes were translated into Italian by Andrea Cambini, about 1490 ; into German by Eugen Wolf, Jena 1927). In one of these disputes with Lorenzo and Giuliano de' Medici Leon Battista Alberti lays down that complete abstention from worldly aims is the best guide to the perfection of personality ; but Lorenzo defends the thesis that only *Active and Contemplative Life*, the two phases of our existence, combined and equilibrating each other, can lead us to the true fulfilment of all the tasks of our human mission. (Reumont, Lorenzo de' Medici, 2nd vol., pp. 43 f., Leipzig 1874.)

brought down fragments three or four fingers in breadth, and so exactly at the point marked, that if only a tiny piece of marble more had fallen, he would have been in danger of ruining the whole work ". From Condivi we learn that he was still working on this group in 1553. In his second edition Vasari says : "At this time (1556) Michelangelo worked on it almost every day as a pastime. At last he broke the stone, probably because it contained many flaws and was so hard that the chisel struck sparks from it ; perhaps also because his judgement was so severe that nothing he did satisfied him. For this reason, to tell the truth, there are few finished works by him from his late period, when he had achieved the highest maturity of his power of artistic creation. His completed statues were all done in his early period ".—Vasari goes on to relate that Michelangelo gave the broken Pietà to Francesco Bandini, who wanted to have it finished by Tiberio Calcagni ; but Calcagni died in 1565. When we see what he did to the work before he died, we must confess that his death was a piece of good fortune. The completely polished and meticulously chiselled Magdalen is his work ; it must have been very beautiful before. He was also responsible for the polishing of the trunk of Christ and for the sharp folds of the shroud (Thode V, 276 f.—Grünwald, Florentiner Studien, p. 14). The additions are harmless : the left forearm of Christ from the elbow to the wrist ; the hand of the Virgin on Christ's left breast and a piece below it ; parts of Christ's right forearm.—Dürer's woodcut of the Holy Trinity influenced this group.—Vasari proposed that the Pietà should be placed on Michelangelo's tomb, according to the master's own intention,[26] but this was not done. For a long time the group was left in the open air, in a vineyard on Monte Cavallo ; it was not until 1722 that it was placed behind the high altar in the cathedral of Florence. The Nicodemus[27] is a self-portrait of Michelangelo (Brinckmann, p. 91.—Symonds II, 201).— Thode (V, 278) says : " I see no reason for doubting Vasari's statement that the master gave his own features to the Nicodemus ".

Thode III, 690 f. ; V, 273 f.—Justi I, 383.—W. R. Valentiner, The Late Years of Michelangelo, New York, 1913.

THE RONDANINI PIETÀ (in the Palazzo Sanseve-rino). Plate 141 (140).—Marble, lifesize.—On February 12th, 1564, six days before his death, Michelangelo worked all day long standing in front of this group. It is possible that the group was originally planned with three figures and that the separate arm is the remains of this hewn-off third figure.[28] Blaise de Vigenère saw the master working on a Deposition with several figures, for which he was using an ancient block of marble from a pillar of Vespasian's temple of peace in Rome (an examination of the marble might throw more light on the question). " The other supporting figures " which Mackowsky assumed, were " certainly not contemplated " according to Brinckmann (p. 94), who speaks of " remodelling ". " The original right arm of the Christ remained in position and was to have been removed later."

Thode III, 690 f. ; V, 278 f. ; 496 f. ; VI, 204.—Mackowsky, p. 306 f.—Max Dvorak, Jahrbuch f. Kunstgesch., Vienna, 1921, p. 26 f.—Panofsky in Festschrift für Friedländer, 1927, p. 273.

THE PALESTRINA PIETÀ. Plate 142 (143, 144). Marble, 88½ inches.—Discovered by A. Grenier in the second side-chapel of the oratory of Santa Rosalia in the Palazzo Barberini, Palestrina (Gazette des Beaux-Arts, XXXVII, 1907, p. 177 f.). Attributed by A. E. Popp to an " imitator of Michelangelo " (Z.f.b.K., new series V, 1924–1925).—" The group is close to the style and conception of his last years, but has not the quality of the works executed by his own hand," was the verdict of F. Schottmüller in her edition of Vasari (VII, 2, p. 417).—Mackowsky (p. 306), however, was unable to understand the doubts as to its authenticity. Since the group, freed from the ugly stucco curtain, has been exhibited at the 1938 exhibition in Rome, it is hardly possible to doubt its authenticity, though it is true that it is not quite free from later revision by other hands, especially as regards the shroud. The Palestrina Pietà has been brought to Florence and placed in the Accademia.[29]

Wallerstein, Z.f.b.K., new series XXV, 1914, p. 325 f.—G. S. Davies, Michelangelo, London 1924, p. 188.

---

[26] In his Life of Baccio Bandinelli Vasari says : " Buonarroti's group consisted of five (?) figures hewn from one block of marble and the master began it with the intention of erecting it above his own tomb in the church of Santa Maria Maggiore ".

[27] St. John xix, 38–40 : "And after this Joseph of Arimathaea . . . besought Pilate that he might take away the body of Jesus : and Pilate gave him leave. . . . And there came also Nicodemus, which at the first came to Jesus by night, and brought a mixture of myrrh and aloes. . . . Then took they the body of Jesus, and wound it in linen clothes with the spices, as the manner of the Jews is to bury."—St. Matthew xxvii, 61 : "And there was Mary Magdalene, and the other Mary, sitting over against the sepulchre "

---

[28] The studies for a sculpture at Oxford (Thode 442, Frey 239, Brinckmann 80, Berenson 1572) show a group of two figures in two of the sketches, but groups of three figures in the other three (dated by Brinckmann about 1560. This drawing is not a reason for assuming that the Rondanini Pietà was begun as early as 1540).

[29] It is proposed to transfer to the Accademia the Michelangelo sculptures from the Museo Nazionale, the Palazzo Vecchio and perhaps from the Casa Buonarroti as well.

ATTRIBUTIONS, LOST WORKS, MODELS

The first work of Michelangelo's mentioned by Condivi is the *Head of a Faun*. The artist was fourteen years old when he made it. Attempts have been made to identify as this work a mask in the Museo Nazionale, Florence, but this has since been recognized as the work of a decadent seventeenth-century master (Knapp, p. 157.—Mackowsky, p. 387.—Justi II, p. 20).—The marble relief of *Apollo and Marsyas* in the Reinhold von Liphart-Rathshoff collection, Munich, is held by Mackowsky to be authentic. (Plate III *c*.) It is an enlarged free copy after an antique cameo of Lorenzo de' Medici's (now in the Museo Nazionale, Naples), and was originally an oval measuring 15¾ by 11¾ inches. If the relief were really by Michelangelo, we should here have preliminary stages for two important works: for the marble David in the Apollo, and for the Captives in the Marsyas. Bode thought that it was an unfinished work by Michelangelo made when he was a boy of fourteen. Thode and Davies likewise uphold its authenticity, but Knapp and in particular Frey have given adequate reasons for rejecting it. (Wilhelm Bode, Jahrbuch der preuss. Kunstsamml. XII, 1891, 167 f.—Bode, Florentiner Bildhauer, Berlin 1921, p. 307 f.—Strzygowski, Jahrb. d. preuss. Kunsts. XII, 1891, p. 210 f.—Knapp, p. 170. —Frey, Quellen I, 91 f.—Mackowsky, p. 387, and Burlington Magazine, LIII, 1928: " Michelangelo's first sculpture ".)—The marble statuette of an *Apollo* in the Kaiser-Friedrich-Museum, Berlin, 30¾ inches high, has been vigorously defended by Bode, who purchased it from the repository of the Villa Borghese, and, curiously enough, included by Knapp among the genuine works as one made by Michelangelo when he was eighteen, but has been rightly eliminated from Michelangelo's œuvre by Frey and Mackowsky (Plate I *d*). A marble statuette in the Victoria and Albert Museum (St. Sebastian, catalogue No. 7561–1861) shows " more than a technical relationship " to this statuette of Apollo; it has recently been attributed to Tribolo (Plate I *c*), but it is probably a school copy after a lost sketch for the Captives for the tomb of Julius (Museum catalogue, p. 132). The Apollo might also be a similar school copy after a lost original.[30] This theory finds support in the freedom of conception combined with inexperienced execution and failure to understand certain parts and also the employment of a technique which is a slavish imitation of Michelangelo's, despite the clumsy use of pointing-iron and dented chisel; the fine conception of form points to a copyist who was actually a

pupil, and not to a beginner who was imitating. (Bode, Jahrb. d. preuss. Kunsts. XXII, p. 88 f.—Bode, Florentiner Bildhauer, p. 311 f.—Frey, Quellen I, p. 98.— Mackowsky, p. 388.)—The *statue of Hercules* which passed from the Palazzo Strozzi into the possession of the King of France, has been lost; nothing has been heard of it since 1713. Michelangelo was seventeen years old when he made this statue, which was a little larger than the " dying captive " in the Louvre. (Justi II, 43 f.—J. P. Richter, Zeitschr. f. bild. Kunst XII, 1877, p. 131.—F. Wickhoff, Mitteil. d. Inst. f. österr. Geschichtsf. III, 1882, p. 421.—Frey, Quellen I, p. 105 f.—Mackowsky, p. 388.)—Another lost work is the *wooden crucifix* which Michelangelo made in the same year for the Prior of Santo Spirito, Florence, and which Thode claimed to recognize in a mediocre work in that church. (Thode V, 18 f. —L. v. Bürkel, Zeitschr. f. bild. Kunst, 1904, p. 297 f.)—Bode believed he had rediscovered the

The wooden Crucifix in Santo Spirito, Florence (not by Michelangelo)

Giovannino or young St. John which Michelangelo made when he was twenty (Plate 1*a*), and Thode, Justi and Frey also supported its authenticity. Wickhoff, Wölfflin, Knapp and Mackowsky reject it and Grünwald suggests that this marble statue (56 inches, now in the museum at Berlin) is the work of the mannerist sculptor Domenico Pieratti, though his grounds for this attribution are unconvincing. Wölfflin proposed the Neapolitan Girolamo Santacroce, and Carlo Gamba, Silvio Cosini, one of Michelangelo's assistants. I think that it is the work of a mediocre Lombard sculptor of the end of the sixteenth century; the marble Bacchus in the Victoria and Albert Museum (Catalogue, No. 218–1879) may be by the same hand. (W. Bode, Jahrb. d. preuss. Kunsts. II, 1881, p. 72 f.—Bode, Florentiner Bildhauer, p. 297 f.—Wölfflin, Jugendwerke, Munich 1891, p. 69 f.— Wölfflin, Klassische Kunst, 3rd edition, Munich 1904, p. 47 f.—Carlo Gamba, Dedalo X, 1929.—Mackowsky, p. 389 f.—Panofsky, col. 26.—Alois Grünwald, Florentiner Studien, Dresden 1914.—Grünwald, Über einige unechte Werke Michelangelos, Münchener Jahrb. d. bild. Kunst I, 1910.)—The extensive restoration[31] of the group of *Bacchus and Ampelus* in the Uffizi at Florence was ascribed by Bayersdorfer to the youthful

---

[30] " The lost Apollo statue must have been similar (to the Drunken Bacchus); it was Michelangelo's second work in Rome, commissioned by a burgher patron, the same who purchased the Bacchus and later gave him the order for the Pietà." (J. Wilde, Mitt. d. kunsthist. Inst. in Florenz, IV, p. 55.)

[31] Only the torso and thighs of the Bacchus are antique.

PLATE   I   Attributed to Michelangelo: a. John the Baptist, Berlin, Kaiser-Friedrich Museum. — b. Bacchus and Ampelus, Florence, Uffizi. — c. Captive (or St. Sebastian), London, Victoria and Albert Museum. — d. Apollo, Berlin, Kaiser-Friedrich-Museum.

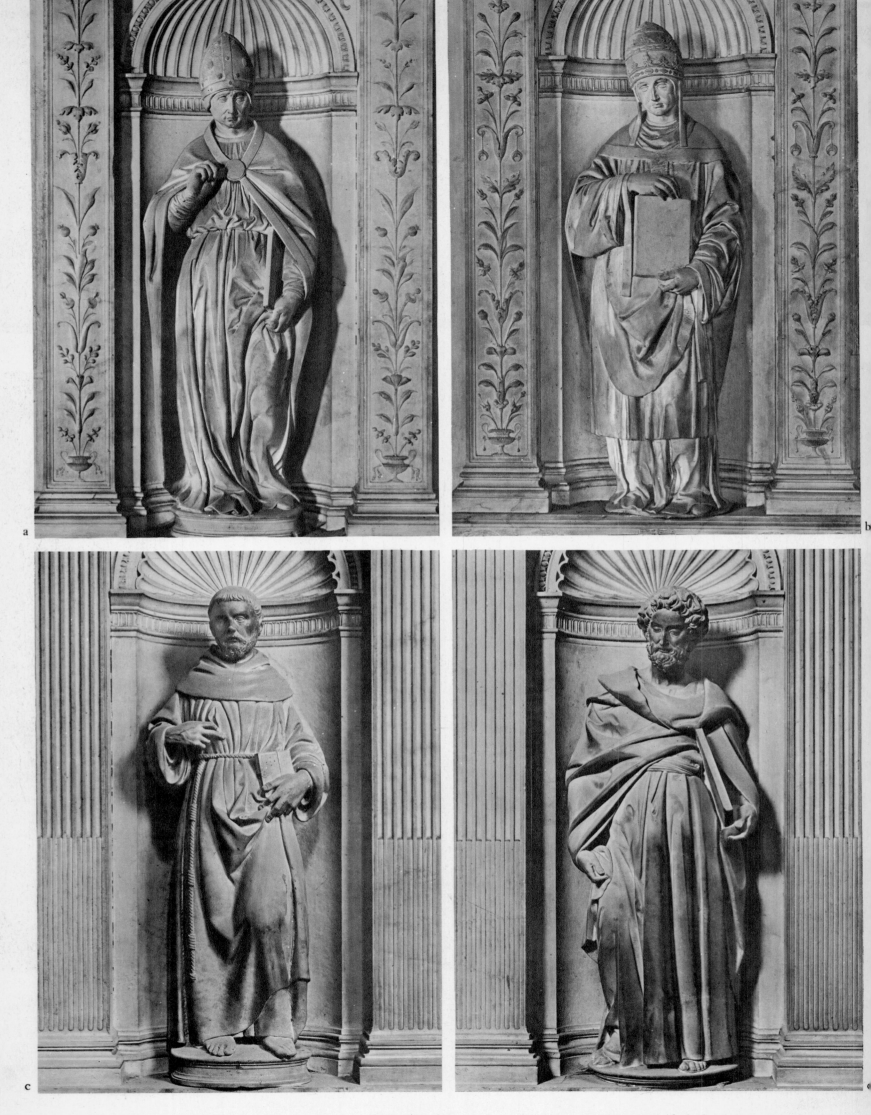

PLATE   II   Michelangelo and assistants: four statues from the Piccolomini altar in the Siena Cathedral, about 1501-1504.
a. St. Gregory.   b. St. Pius.   c. St. Francis.   d. St. James.

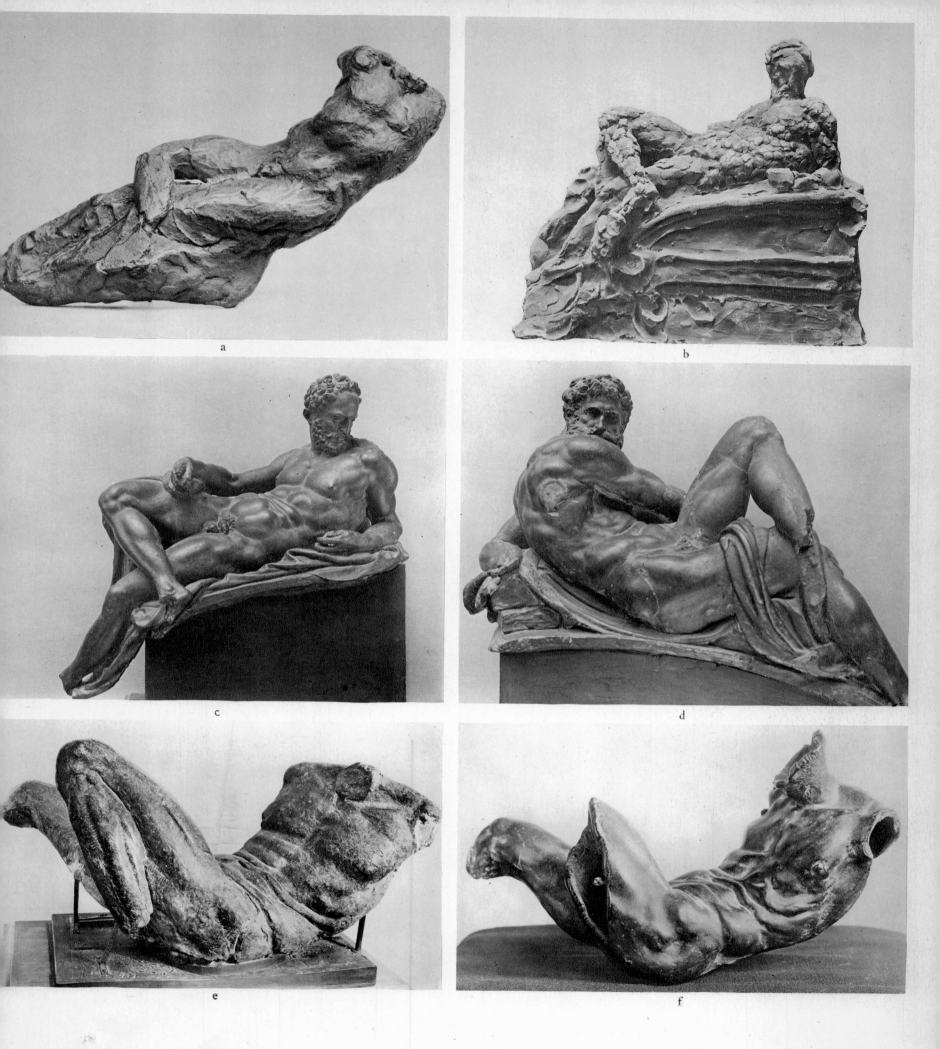

PLATE VII   a. and b.   Wax sketches by Michelangelo for the " Crepusculo " (a) London, British Museum; (b) Florence, Accademia.—
c. and d. Wax models after the " Crepusculo " and " Giorno " (by Vincenzo Danti ?) Florence, Accademia. —
e. and f. Ammanati, after Michelangelo : River god. (e) Clay, Florence, Accademia. (f) bronze, Florence, Museo Nazionale.

PLATE VIII   Deposition, about 1540, stucco derived from a lost wax relief by Michelangelo, Florence, Casa Buonarroti.

Michelangelo (Plate 1 *b*), but Grünwald has shown that the additions were executed about 1590 by Giovanni Cinelli. (Walther Amelung, Führer durch die Antiken von Florenz, p. 76.—Wölfflin, Jugendwerke, p. 76.—Mackowsky, p. 390.)—According to Thode (III, p. 112; VI, p. 287) the *dying Adonis* in the Museo Nazionale Florence, was begun about 1496 by Michelangelo and finished later by Vincenzo Rossi. This ugly work was

Dying Adonis, marble, by Vincenzo Rossi (?), Florence, Museo Nazionale

rejected by Herman Grimm; Schlosser claimed that it was the work of Vincenzo Danti; Grünwald made a thorough study of it and declared it to be by Rossi. (Grünwald, Florentiner Studien.—A. E. Brinckmann, Monatshefte, f. Kunstwissensch. XIII, 1920, p. 324).—Condivi mentions two *statues of Cupid* executed by Michelangelo between his return from Bologna and the time when he was working on the Bacchus (i.e. 1495–1497). The first version represented a *sleeping Cupid* and was sold to Cardinal Riario as a genuine antique; it was thus a bogus antique. This statue later came into the possession of Isabella d'Este, Margravine of Mantua. The Anonimo Morelliano mentions a sleeping Cupid

in the house of Pietro Bembo at Padua, " different from the copy belonging to the Duchess Isabella d'Este ". Konrad Lange believed he had rediscovered this early work of Michelangelo in an indifferent exhibit in the Turin museum. A more likely suggestion is that there is a reproduction of this lost work in a painting by Giulio Romano, who worked at the Mantuan court from 1525, and another in a picture by Tintoretto, of whom we know that he collected reproductions of Michelangelo's works. (K. Lange, Der schlafende Amor des Michelangelo, Leipzig 1898.—A. Bayersdorfer, Leben und Schriften, Munich 1902, p. 112.—Mackowsky, p. 391.—Johannes Wilde, Mitt. d. kunsthist. Inst. in Florenz, IV, 1932, p. 53.)—*The second version of the Cupid*, that is to say, the one made for Jacopo Galli, has been identified by some as the Cupid now in the Victoria and Albert Museum (*cf*. note to Plate 17).—By a contract made in June 1501 Michelangelo undertook to deliver five statues 45 inches high for the *Piccolomini Altar* in the cathedral at Siena. " It may be assumed ", says Mackowsky (p. 395), " that Michelangelo left most of this for him not very attractive order to his subordinates ". Of the fifteen statues on the altar, however, four or five are derived from his designs; the St. Gregory and St. Peter are perhaps the most akin to his manner, while the right arm of St. James has distant reminiscences of the David. In Tolnai's opinion only the St. James is by Michelangelo's own hand, and the remaining statues were executed by assistants. Johannes Wilde describes the altar as " entirely due to Michelangelo, the assistants having merely given the finishing touches ".—

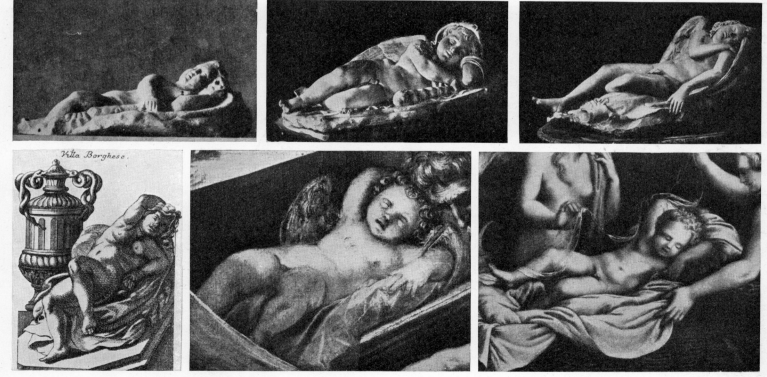

Sleeping Cupid, copies after antique sculptures.—1. *Rome, Museo Vaticano.*—2. *and* 3. *Turin, Museo di Antichità.*—
4. *Antique sculpture, Rome, Villa Borghese, copper engraving after Montfaucon.*—5. *Detail from Tintoretto's " Mars and Venus ", about 1545, Munich, Pinakothek.*—
6. *Detail from Giulio Romano's " The Infancy of Jupiter ", about 1535, London, National Gallery*

From the end of November 1506 to the end of February 1508 Michelangelo was busy with the casting of his *bronze statue of Pope Julius II* in Bologna after the city had been subjugated by the Pope. The first casting was unsuccessful, as the statue emerged from the furnace only as far as the girdle; but by February 15th, 1508, it was finished. The statue was over ten feet high and weighed about seventeen tons. The Pope was represented seated, with Peter's keys in his left hand and his right raised in the act of benediction; it may have resembled the (supposedly early Christian) seated bronze statue of

St. Peter, marble, from the Piccolomini altar, Siena, Cathedral, about 1501–1504

St. Peter in St. Peter's at Rome.[32] The statue remained above the main portal of San Petronio for only three years and nine months; then the populace of Bologna rising in defence of its freedom, pulled the statue down and destroyed it. Duke Alfonso of Ferrara caused a mighty cannon to be cast from the pieces, which he ironically called "La Giulia". The portrait head which was preserved by the Duke in his art cabinet as the only relic of this work of Michelangelo's, has likewise disappeared. The destruction of the statue of Julius is the most serious loss we have suffered among Michelangelo's works. (Thode, IV, 118 f.—W. Hager, Die Ehrenstatuen der Päpste, Leipzig 1929.)— Before this there was another bronze sculpture by Michelangelo, the life-size *bronze David* which was commissioned in

Seated figure of St. Peter, bronze, Rome, St. Peter's (copy after the Early Christian marble statue which stood above the portal of the old basilica of St. Peter)

1. *Verrocchio, David, bronze, about 1465, Florence, Museo Nazionale.*—2. *Bertoldo, Hercules, bronze, about 1480, Berlin, Museum.*—3. *Donatello, David, bronze, about 1430, Berlin, Museum*

1502, sent to France via Leghorn in 1508 and has been lost for the last three hundred years (Plate IV). The commission stipulated expressly that this bronze David should be similar to the bronze by Donatello (*cf.* above fig. 3). *Two wax models in the Casa Buonarroti and the Victoria and Albert Museum, a bronze statuette in the Louvre and one in Amsterdam* have been connected with this bronze David; but these suppositions have been contradicted. (On the model in Florence: Thode III, 183; IV, 79; VI, 279.—On the model in London: Thode, IV, 89; VI, 283. Catalogue of Italian Sculpture in the Victoria and Albert Museum, 1932, p. 131.—On the Paris statuette: Courajod, Gaz. archéol. X, 185, p. 77 f.; Thode III, 180 f.; IV, 88; VI, 295.—On the Amsterdam statuette, A. Pitt, Revue d'art ancien et moderne 1897, 78 and 455. Thode III, 182; IV, 86 f.).—Jan Six (Gazette des Beaux-Arts LXIII, 1921, p. 166 f.) has attributed to the same period as the bronze David the large *bronze Apollo* in the Louvre, which A. E. Popp on the other hand (Die Medicikapelle Michelangelos, Munich 1922) held to be the Apollo executed for Baccio Valori about 1529–1530. Panofsky (Die Michelangelo-Literatur, Vienna 1922, col. 57) calls the Louvre bronze "the work of a rather indifferent eclectic" and assumes for it a French origin.[33] It is to be hoped that this work will soon cease to be a subject of discussion.[34]—The *relief of St. Andrew* (Plate IIIa and b) which we mentioned in connection with the St. Matthew (Plate 50), could, if it were authentic, only be ascribed to the period of the second order for the cathedral. Of this order Andrea Ferrucci da Fiesole undertook the execution of the St. Andrew (*cf.* note 10). The relief is probably the sketched out base for the statue, and thus by the hand of Andrea

---

[32] Among the works left by Michelangelo after his death there was an unfinished statue of a seated St. Peter (since lost) which Vasari in a letter to the master's nephew calls "the portrait of the Pope". Perhaps this may actually have been a marble bozzetto of "Pope Julius as Peter", a design for the bronze likeness, and not the figure of the Pope intended for his tomb. (Thode I, 477; V, 283.)

---

[33] I believe it to be by Pierre Francheville (1548–1618), active in Rome, Florence and elsewhere, who is well represented in the Louvre by the bronze Captives for Giovanni da Bologna's monument to Henri IV and by several marble sculptures, such as the "David" and "Orpheus".

[34] The Apollo made for Valori was in marble (not bronze, like this statue) and about 67 inches high (not over 6 ft. 6 in.).

Ferrucci. The latter often worked with Michelangelo: in 1517 (probably just before the last statues were ordered for the cathedral, when the St. Matthew, according to Vasari, was entrusted to Michelangelo) he carried out for Michelangelo the foundation of the façade for San Lorenzo; in 1524 he supervised the building of the walls of the Medici chapel. In view of this close colla-boration, it is hardly likely that Andrea Fer-rucci would not at times have been influenced by Michelangelo. This would explain the michelangelesque forms in the St. Andrew relief, in itself a weak work, and this led Dami to attri-bute it to Michelangelo. (L. Dami, Dedalo VII, 1926, p. 29 f.)—The two models for a *river-god*,

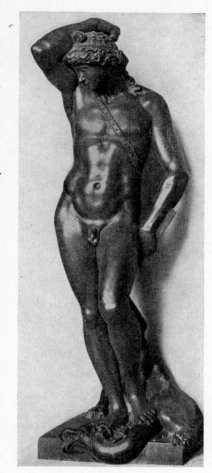

Apollo, bronze (by Pierre Francheville ?), Paris, Louvre

intended for the Medici chapel, are attributed to Bartolomeo Ammanati. (Gottschewski, Zeitschr. f. bildende Kunst, 1906, p. 189 f.—Steinmann, *ibid.*, p. 39.—Thode IV, p. 490 f.; VI, 279.) Both the large clay model and the small one in bronze are supposed to be copies of lost models by Michelangelo (Plates VII, *e* and *f*).—These, like all other *models* in wax and clay ascribed to Michelangelo, have still to be investigated thoroughly; the list which would remain after such a study would be a small one. (Thode VI, 265 f.—Popp, in Medicikapelle, discusses the Edinburgh model.—Burger, Studien zu Michelangelo, 1907, p. 40 f., and Meier-Graefe, Michelangelo: Die Terrakotten aus der Sammlung Hähnel, 1924, deal with the Dresden models.

—On the pieces in the British Museum, see Sir C. J. Holmes, Burlington Magazine, XI, 1907, p. 189.—The models in the Victoria and Albert Museum are best dealt with by Sir Eric Maclagan in the 1932 catalogue, p. 127 f., and also in the Burlington Magazine XLIV, 1924, p. 4 f.; details in Brinckmann, Barock-Bozzetti.) All models are doubtful, even those for the David in the Casa Buonarroti. The same applies to the designs for the *Hercules and Cacus*, of which there is a stucco model in the Casa Buonarroti and a wax one in the Victoria and Albert Museum (Plate V *a* and *b*). Springer thought that they were for a " Victory " group for the tomb of Julius. (Thode V, 297.—J. Wilde, Jahrb. d. kunsthist. Samml. in Wien, new series II, 1928, p. 199 f.). Accord-ing to Vasari the group was subsequently amplified by the addition of a third figure and was intended for Samson's victory over the Philistines. Bronze statuettes after this second design may be seen in the Museo Nazionale, Florence, and elsewhere. Like Springer before him and Wilde subsequently, Justi (II, p. 289 f.) connected the Hercules and Cacus group with the Victory (Plate 81); in his opinion the Florentine model is more likely to have been for the Samson, and in this he is followed by Knapp (p. 166). (Thode III, 470 f.—A. E. Popp, Zeitschr. f. bild. Kunst LVIII, 1924, p. 133.—Brinckmann, Belvedere XI, 1927, p. 155 f.—Tietze-Conrat, Jahrb. d. Kunsthist. Samml. in Wien XII, 1918, p. 57 f.—Panofsky, col. 5.)—Whether the mention in the inventory of Michelangelo's estate on February 19th, 1564, of a small statue (" non finita ") of *Christ bearing the Cross* may have been a design for the statue in Santa Maria sopra Minerva (Plate 85), it is impossible to say. In any case it must have been a particular version, for in 1564 Daniele da Volterra described it as " similar to the Christ in the Minerva, yet differing from it ". (Thode V, 172.) The stucco relief of a *Deposition* in the Casa Buonarroti is held to be a cast after a lost wax relief made by Michelangelo about 1540 (Plate VIII); other copies in wax, ivory and silver have been preserved. (Thode V, 482.—A. E. Brinckmann, Michelangelo-Zeichnungen, Munich 1925, Plate 9 and p. 54.)

THE REPRODUCTIONS

PHOTOGRAPHS BY J. SCHNEIDER-LENGYEL · VANVE-SUR-SEINE · FRANCE

1. MADONNA OF THE STAIRS. ABOUT 1491. FLORENCE, MUSEO BUONARROTI

2. MADONNA OF THE STAIRS. DETAIL FROM PLATE 1

3. THE DEJANIRA RELIEF.   DETAIL FROM PLATE 4

4. THE RAPE OF DEJANIRA. ABOUT 1492 FLORENCE, MUSEO BUONARROTI

5. THE DEJANIRA RELIEF. DETAIL FROM PLATE 4

6. THE DEJANIRA RELIEF. DETAIL FROM PLATE 4

7. THE DEJANIRA RELIEF. DETAIL FROM PLATE 4

10. PROCULUS.   DETAIL FROM PLATE 8

11. HEAD OF PROCULUS. DETAIL FROM PLATE 8

12. HEAD OF THE ANGEL WITH A CANDLESTICK. DETAIL FROM PLATE 16

13-15. KNEELING ANGEL WITH A CANDLESTICK. 1494-1495. BOLOGNA, SAN DOMENICO

16. KNEELING ANGEL WITH A CANDLESTICK. 1494-1495. BOLOGNA, SAN DOMENICO

18. HEAD OF THE CUPID. DETAIL FROM PLATE 17

19. BACCHUS. ABOUT 1497.
FLORENCE, MUSEO NAZIONAL

20. BACCHUS. DETAIL FROM PLATE 19

21. BACCHUS. DETAIL FROM PLATE 19

22. BACCHUS. DETAIL FROM PLATE 19

24. HEAD OF THE MADONNA. DETAIL FROM PLATE 23

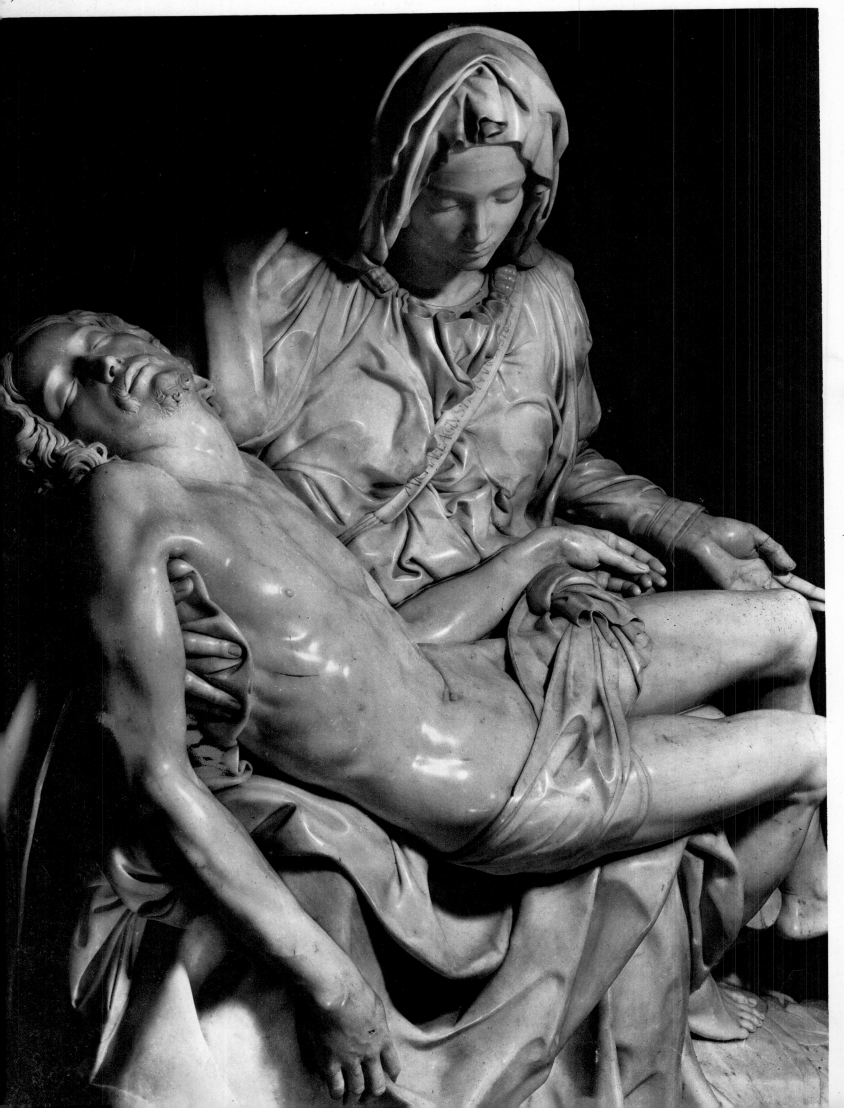

26. HEAD OF CHRIST. DETAIL FROM PLATE 23

27. HEAD OF THE MADONNA. DETAIL FROM PLATE 23

29. LEFT HAND OF CHRIST. DETAIL FROM PLATE 23

30. FEET OF THE INFANT JESUS. DETAIL FROM PLATE 31

31. MADONNA AND CHILD. 1500-1503. BRUGES, NOTRE-DAME

32. HEAD OF THE MADONNA.   DETAIL FROM PLATE 31

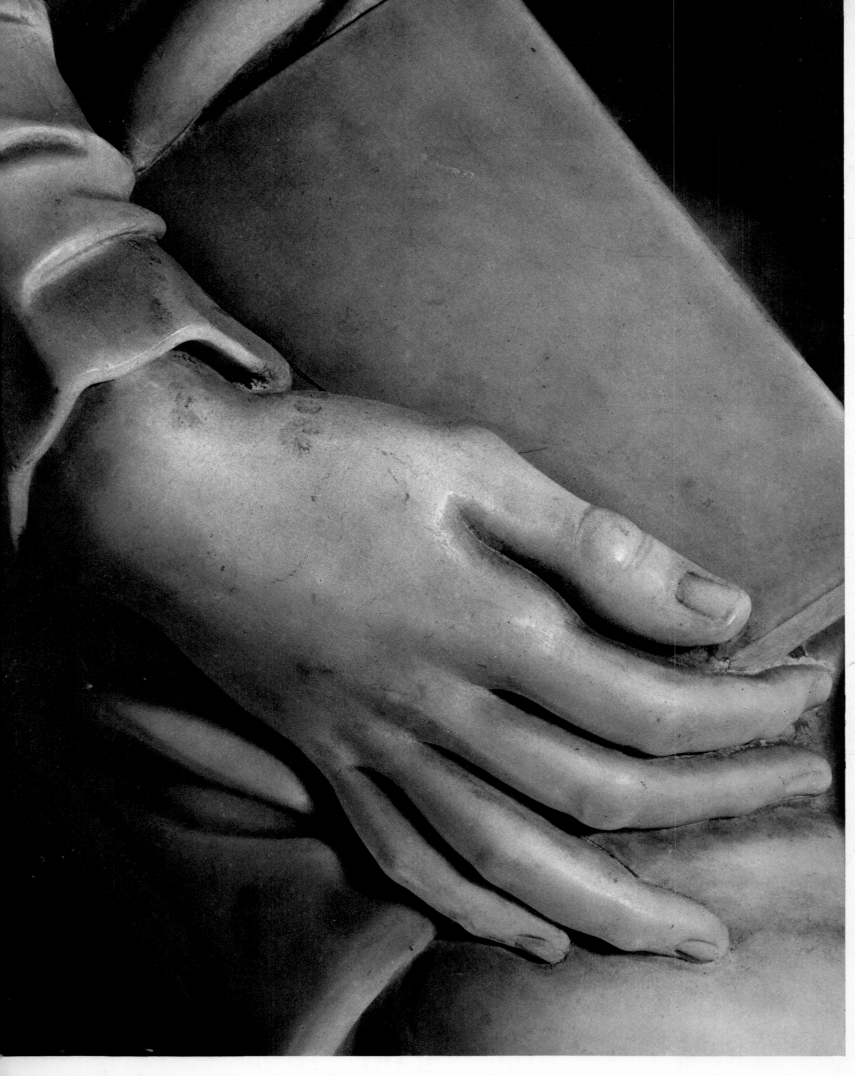

33. RIGHT HAND OF THE MADONNA. DETAIL FROM PLATE 31

34. THE INFANT JESUS. DETAIL FROM PLATE 31

35. HEAD OF THE MADONNA.   DETAIL FROM PLATE 31

37. DAVID.
FLORENCE, ACCADEMIA DI BELLE ART

38. RIGHT HAND OF DAVID.
(OPPOSITE PAGE) DETAIL FROM PLAT

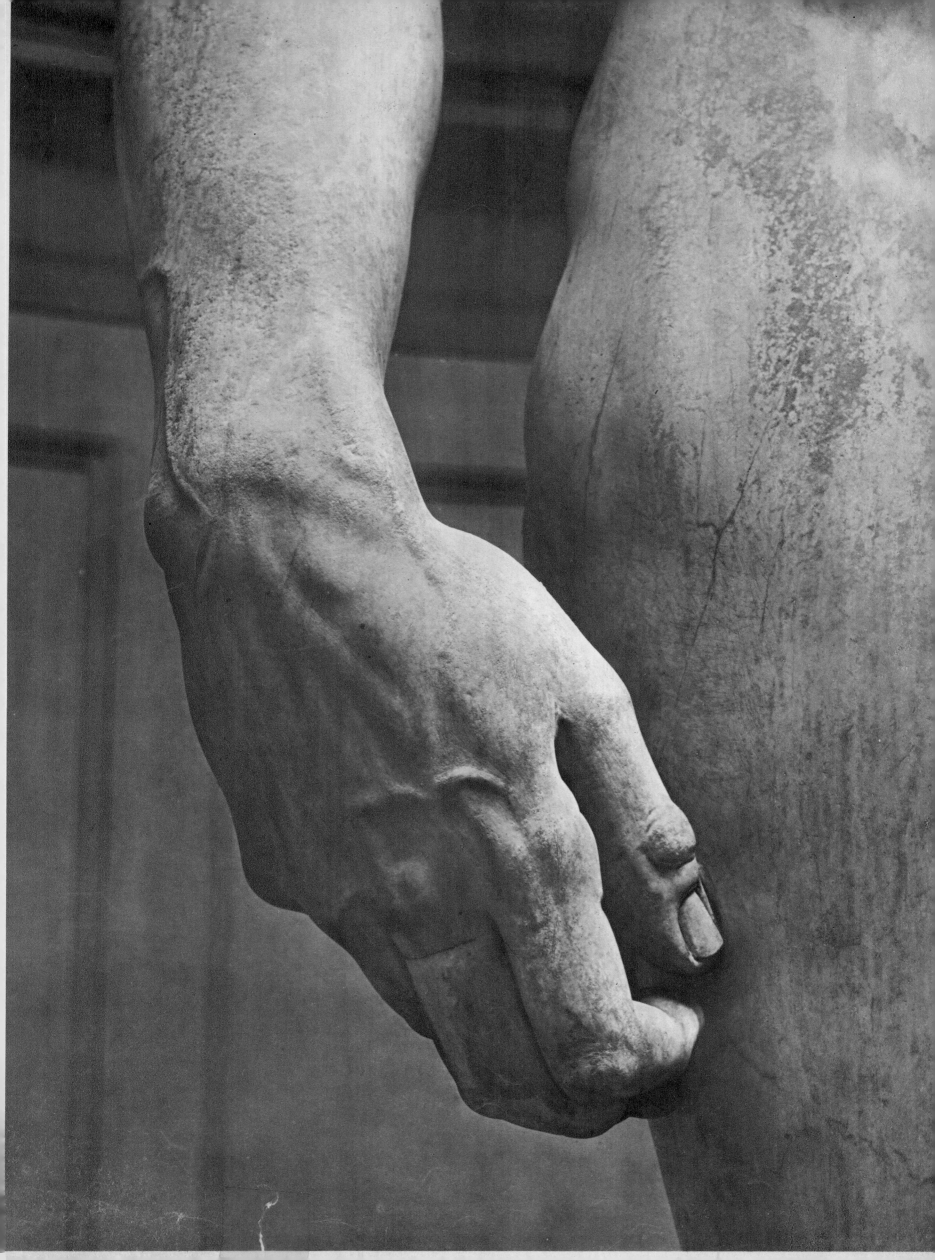

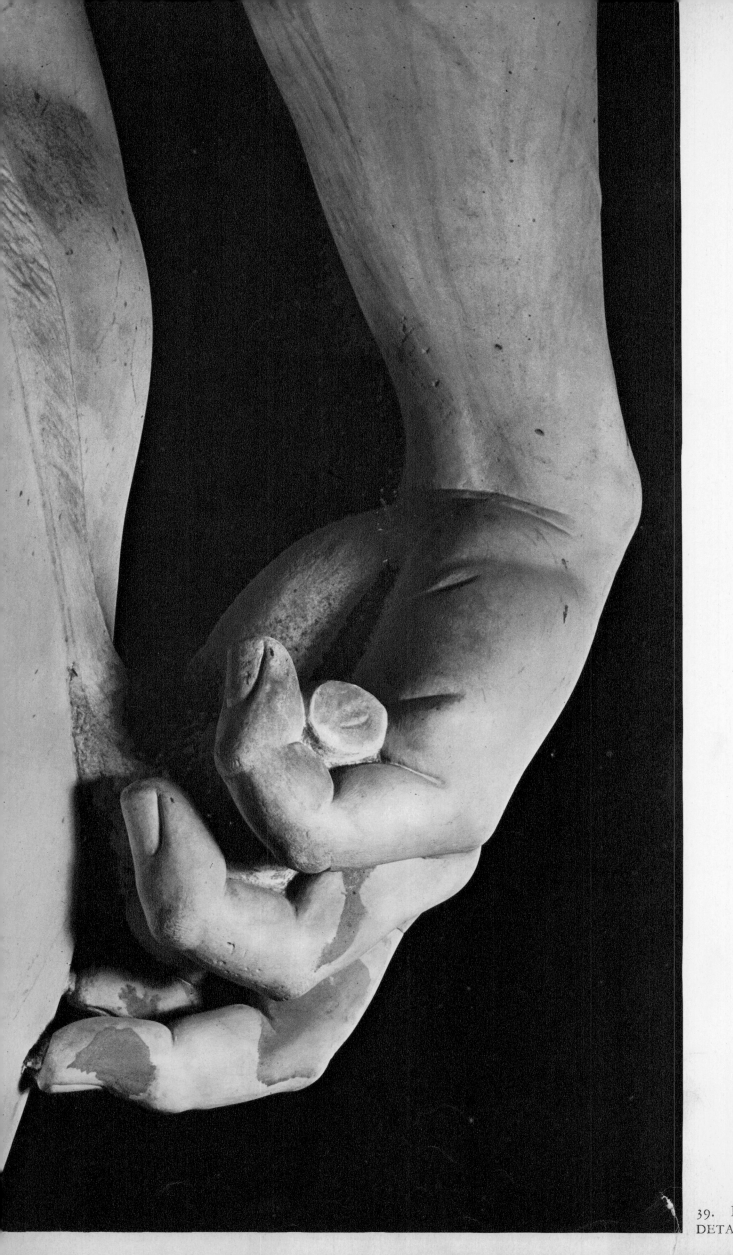

39. RIGHT HAND OF DAVID
DETAIL FROM PLATE 37

40. DAVID. BACK VIEW

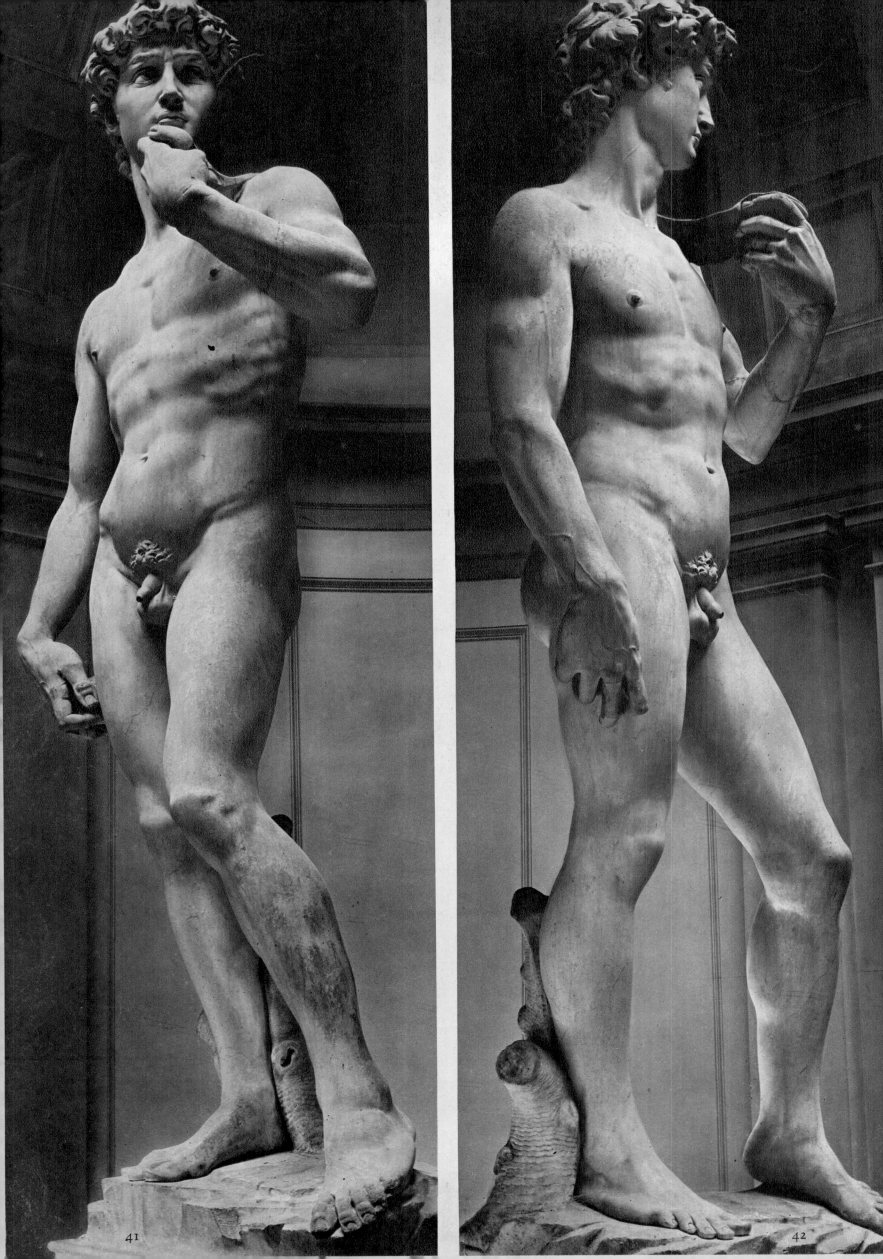

41

42

41-43. DAVID AND HEAD OF DAVID. (CF. PLATE 37)

44. HEAD OF THE MADONNA. DETAIL FROM PLATE 45

5. MADONNA WITH CHILD AND LITTLE SAINT JOHN. ABOUT 1504. FLORENCE, MUSEO NAZIONALE

46. HEAD OF THE INFANT JESUS. DETAIL FROM PLATE 45

47. HEAD OF THE INFANT JESUS. DETAIL FROM PLATE 48

8. MADONNA WITH CHILD AND LITTLE SAINT JOHN.   ABOUT 1504.   LONDON, ROYAL ACADEMY

49. HEAD OF THE MADONNA. DETAIL FROM PLATE 48

50. SAINT MATTHEW.

UNFINISHED. 1504-1506 (?) FLORENCE, ACCADEMIA DI BELLE A[

51. HEAD OF SAINT MATTHEW.   DETAIL FROM PLATE 50

52-53. MOSES. 1513-1516.
ROME, SAN PIETRO IN VINCOLI

54. LEFT HAND OF MOSES.   DETAIL FROM PLATE 52

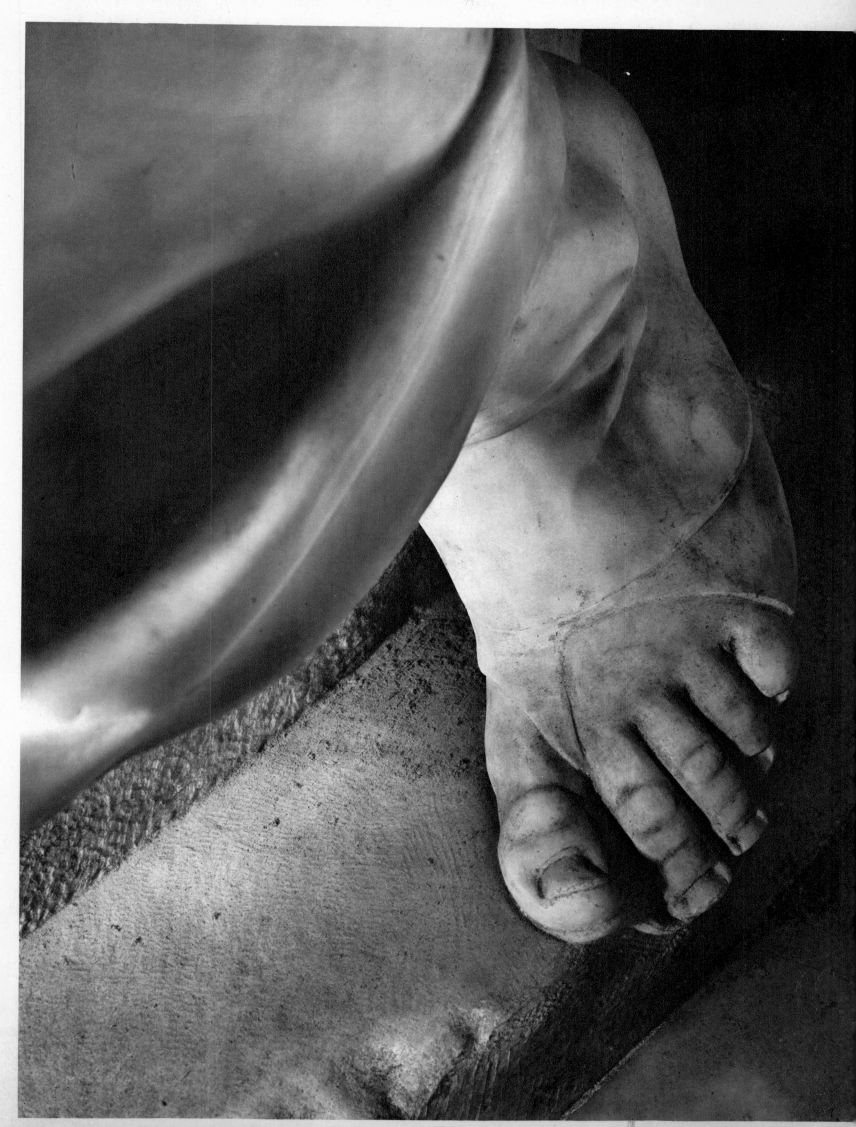

56-57. HEAD OF MOSES.   DETAIL FROM PLATE 52

58. RIGHT HAND OF MOSES. DETAIL FROM PLATE 52

59. RIGHT HAND OF THE DYING CAPTIVE.   DETAIL FROM PLATE 60

60-62.   THE DYING CAPTIVE.   1513-1516.   PARIS, LOUVRE

63. HEAD OF THE DYING CAPTIVE. DETAIL FROM PLATE 60

65-67. THE HEROIC CAPTIVE. 1513-1516. PARIS, LOUVRE

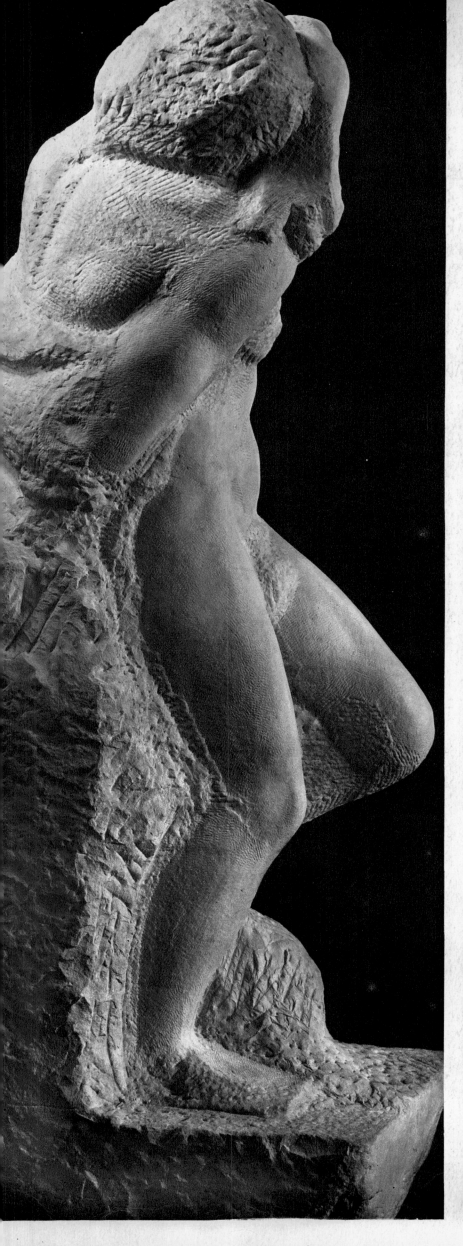

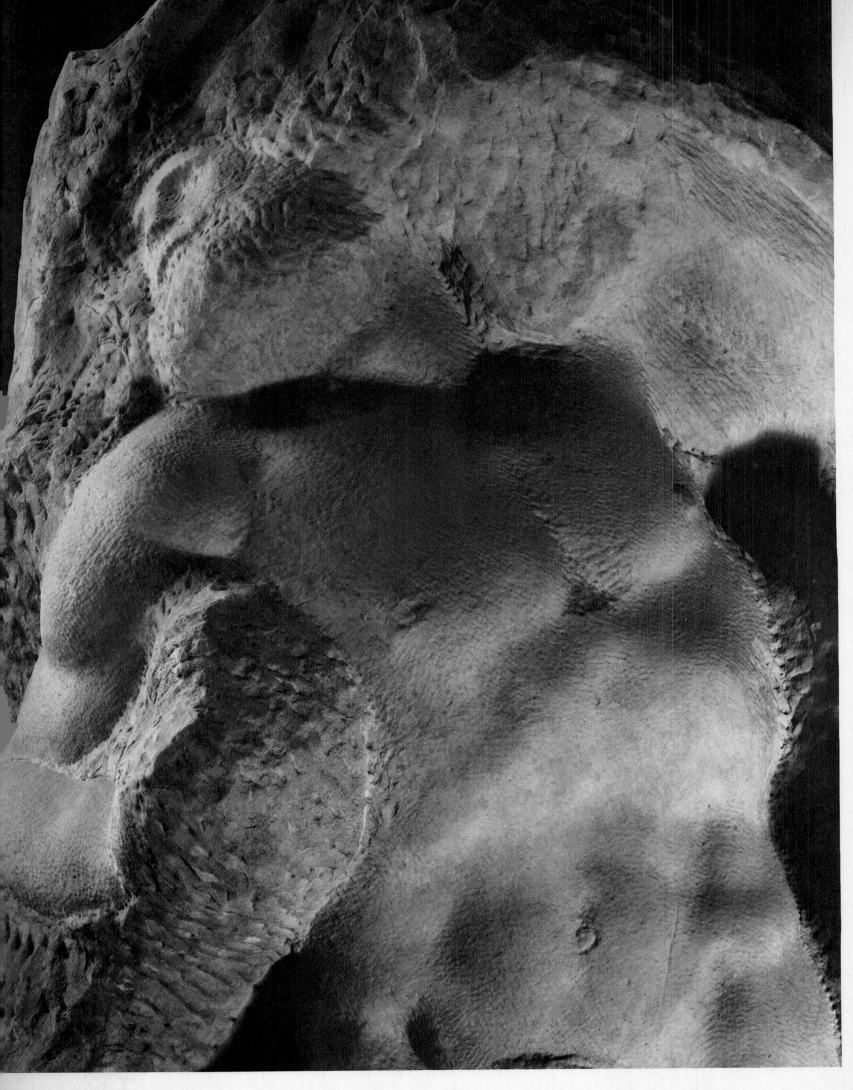

68-75. THE FOUR CAPTIVES FROM THE BOBOLI GARDENS. AFTER 1519. (UNFINISHED), FLORENCE,
    ACADEMIA DI BELLE ARTI

76. CAPTIVE. DETAIL FROM PLATE 71

77. CAPTIVE. DETAIL FROM PLATE 68

78. CAPTIVE. DETAIL FROM PLATE 68

83. HEAD OF THE VICTOR. DETAIL FROM PLATE 81

84. HEAD OF THE VICTOR. DETAIL FROM PLATE 81

87.　HEAD OF CHRIST.　DETAIL FROM PLATE 86

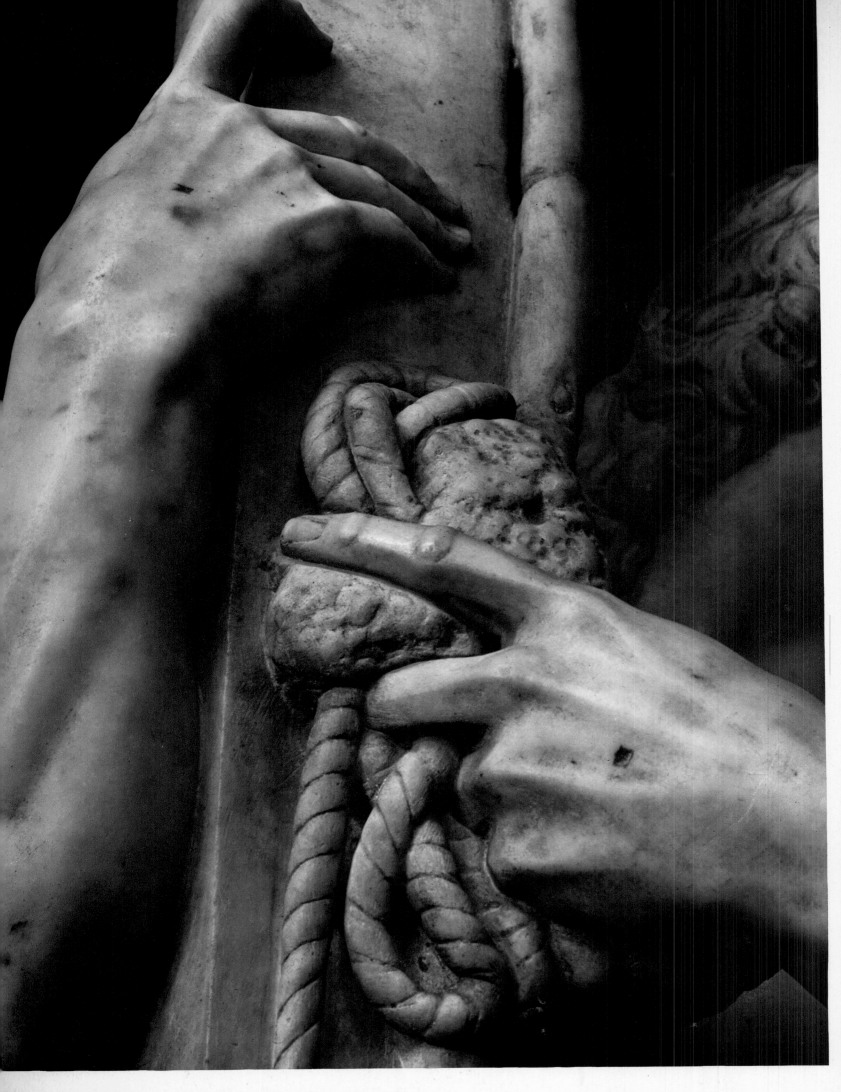

88. THE HANDS OF CHRIST. DETAIL FROM PLATE 85

89. THE MEDICEAN MADONNA. DETAIL FROM PLATE 90

91. HEAD OF THE MEDICEAN MADONNA. DETAIL FROM PLATE 90

92. HEAD OF THE MEDICEAN MADONNA. DETAIL FROM PLATE 90

94. TOMB OF GIULIANO DE' MEDICI. 1521-153
FLORENCE, SAN LORENZO

95. TOMB OF LORENZO DE' MEDICI. 1521-153
FLORENCE, SAN LORENZO

98.   HEAD OF GIULIANO DE' MEDICI.   DETAIL FROM PLATE 97

99. HEAD OF LORENZO DE' MEDICI. DETAIL FROM PLATE 96

100. NIGHT. (LA NOTTE). 1525-1531. DETAIL FROM PLATE 94

101. DAY. (IL GIORNO). 1525-1534. DETAIL FROM PLATE 94

102. EVENING. (IL CREPUSCULO). 1524-1531. DETAIL FROM PLATE 95

Lorenzo

3. DAWN. (L'AURORA). 1524-1531. DETAIL FROM PLATE 95

104. L'AURORA. DETAIL FROM PLATE 103

Dawn - Lorenzo

105. LA NOTTE. DETAIL FROM PLATE 100

106. IL GIORNO. DETAIL FROM PLATE 101

Day - Tomb of Giuliano.

107. LA NOTTE. DETAIL FROM PLATE 100

Night. Giuliano

108. IL GIORNO. DETAIL FROM PLATE 101 *Giuliano*

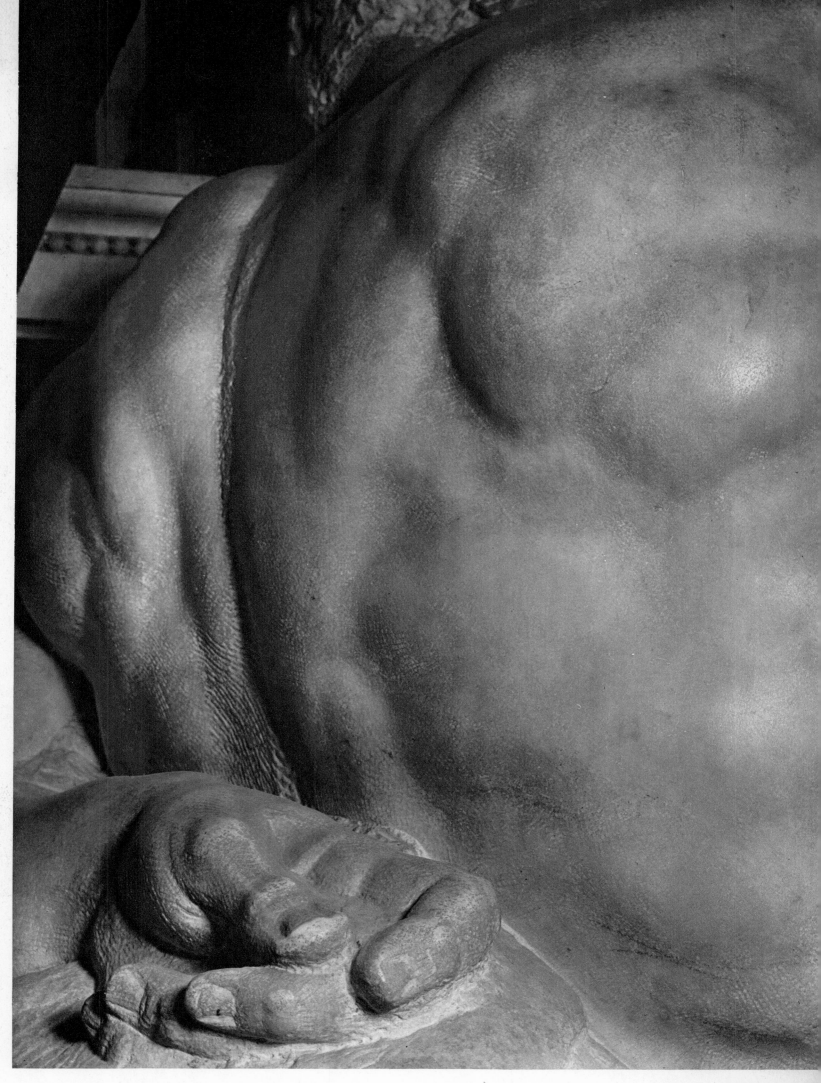

109. IL GIORNO. DETAIL FROM PLATE 101 *Giuliano*

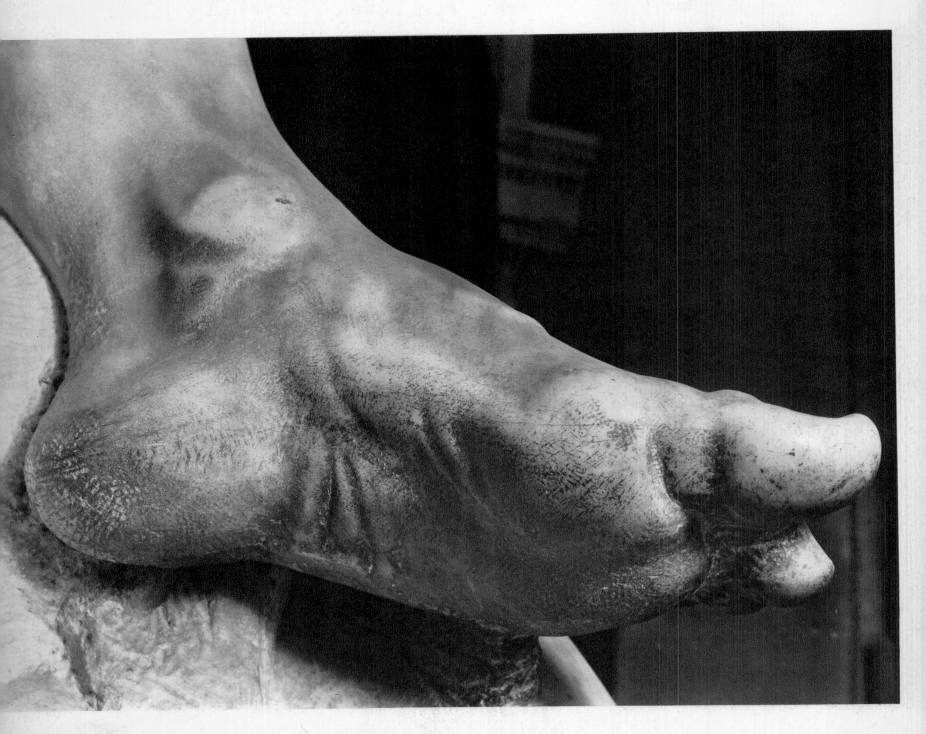

110. LEFT FOOT OF IL GIORNO. DETAIL FROM PLATE 101

Giuliano

111. LEFT HAND OF IL GIORNO.   DETAIL FROM PLATE 101

Giuliano

113.   HEAD OF LA NOTTE.   DETAIL FROM PLATE 100   *Giuliano*

Night

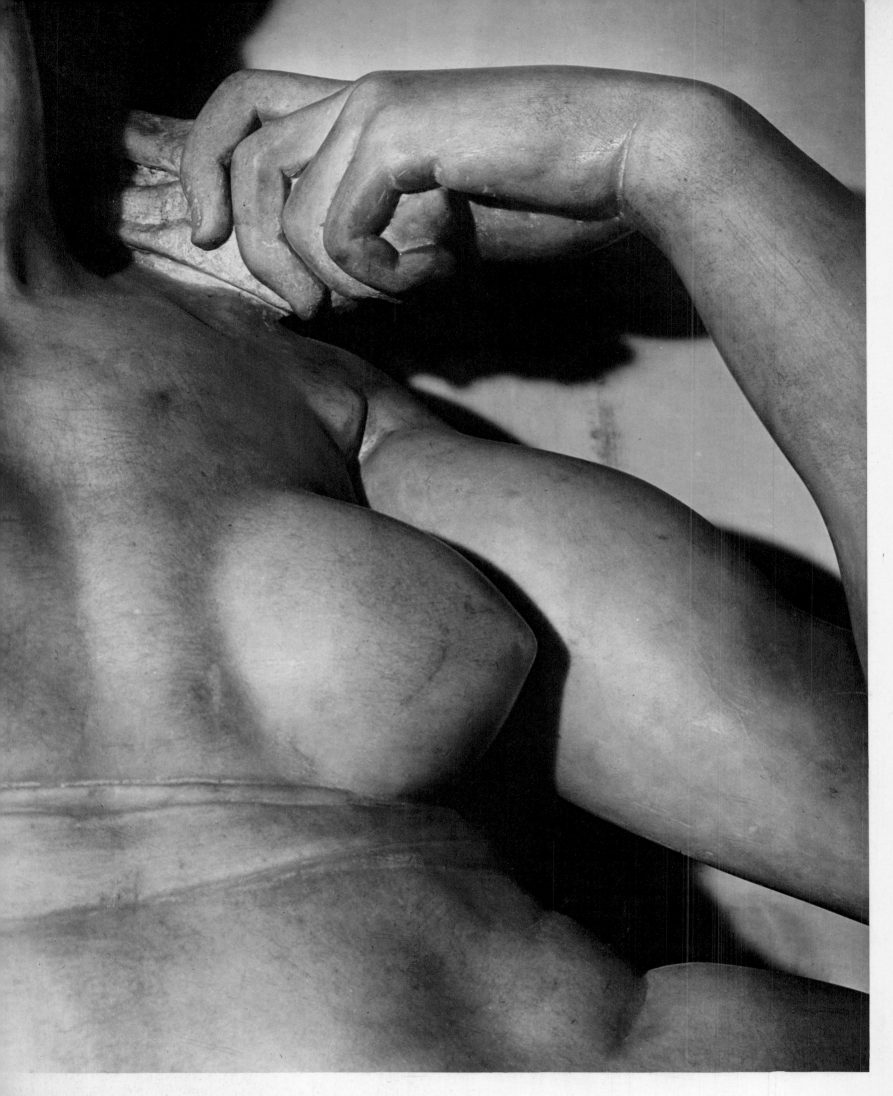

114. LEFT ARM OF L'AURORA. DETAIL FROM PLATE 103

Dawn Lorenzo

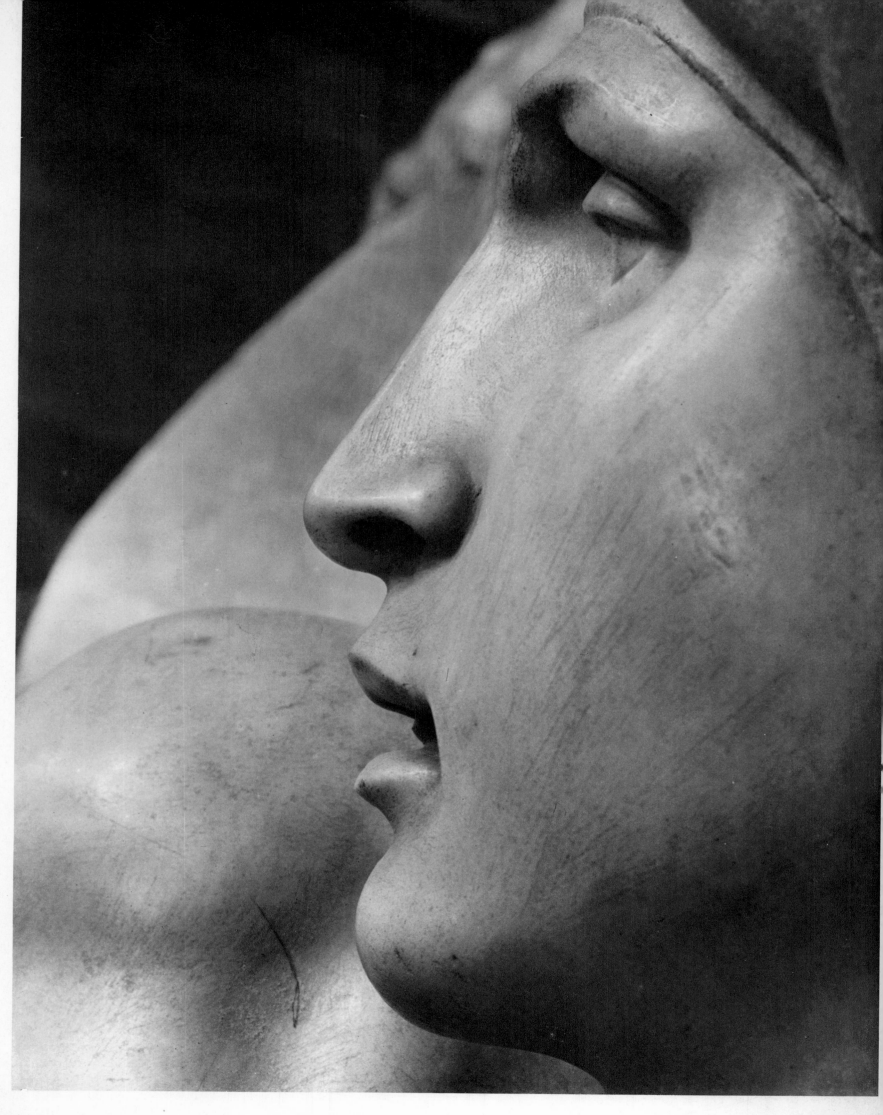

115. HEAD OF L'AURORA.   DETAIL FROM PLATE 103

Dawn - Lorenzo.

116. HEAD OF IL CREPUSCULO. DETAIL FROM PLATE 102

117. HEAD OF L'AURORA. DETAIL FROM PLATE 103

Dawn : Lorenzo

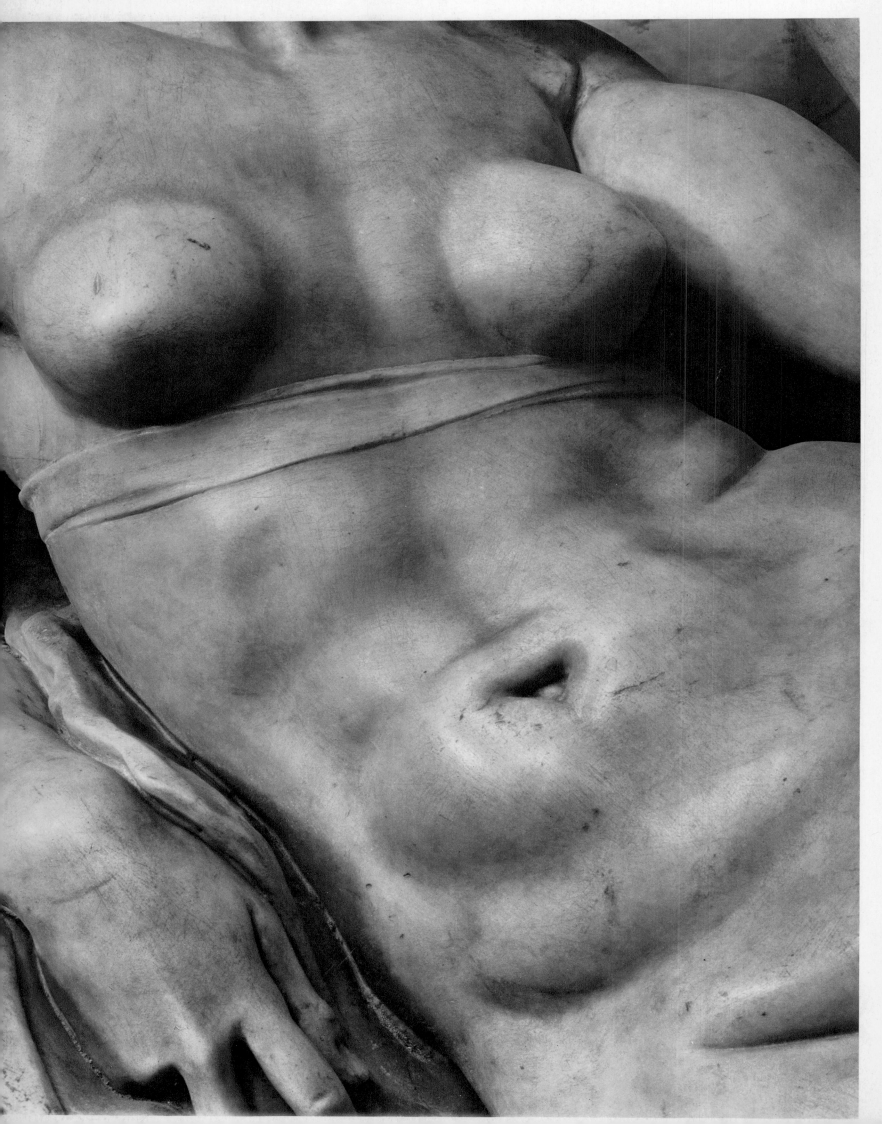

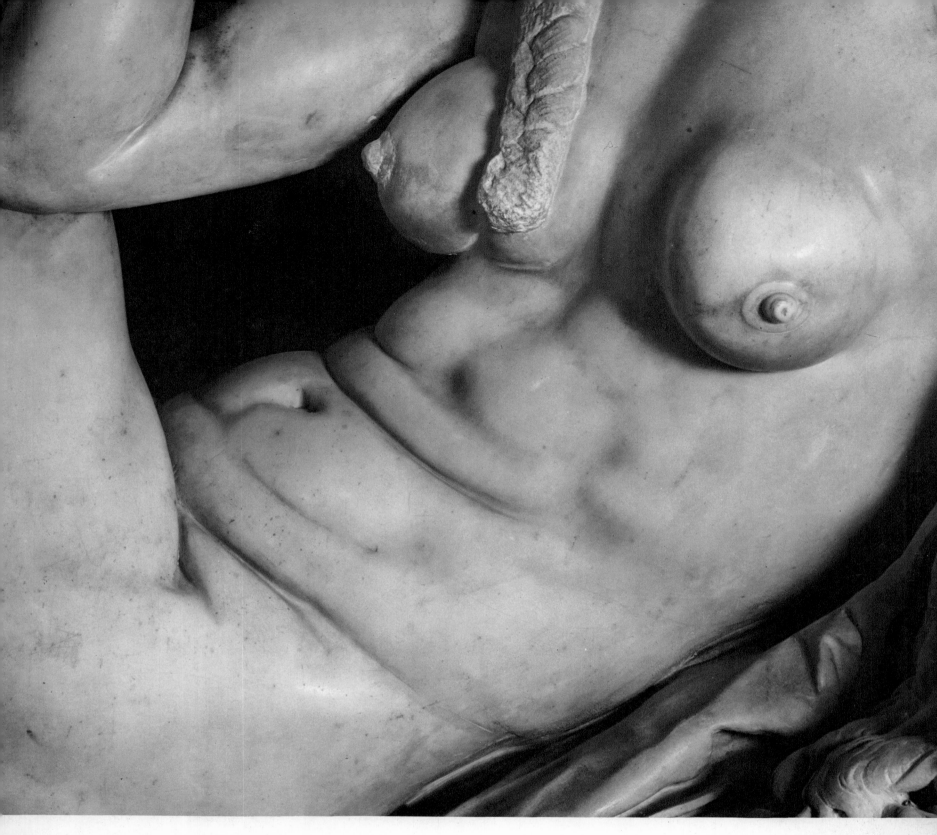

LA NOTTE. DETAIL FROM PLATE 100

120. THE OWL OF LA NOTTE. DETAIL FROM PLATE 100

121.   THE MASK OF LA NOTTE.   DETAIL FROM PLATE 100

122. THE MASK OF THE BACCHUS. DETAIL FROM PLATE 19

HIE·SAVLIV

124. CROUCHING BOY. 1530-1534. LENINGRAD, HERMITAGE

128. APOLLO. DETAIL FROM PLATE 126

129. BRUTUS. ABOUT 1540. FLORENCE, MUSEO NAZIONALE

130. BRUTUS. DETAIL FROM PLATE 129

131. BRUTUS.   DETAIL FROM PLATE 129

132. BRUTUS. DETAIL FROM PLATE 129

133-134.   ACTIVE AND CONTEMPLATIVE LIFE.   1542-1543.   ROME, SAN PIETRO IN VINCOLI

138. MICHELANGELO'S SELF-PORTRAIT.   DETAIL FROM PLATE 137

139. HEADS OF NICODEMUS AND CHRIST. DETAIL FROM PLATE 137

140. HEADS OF MARY AND CHRIST. DETAIL FROM PLATE 141

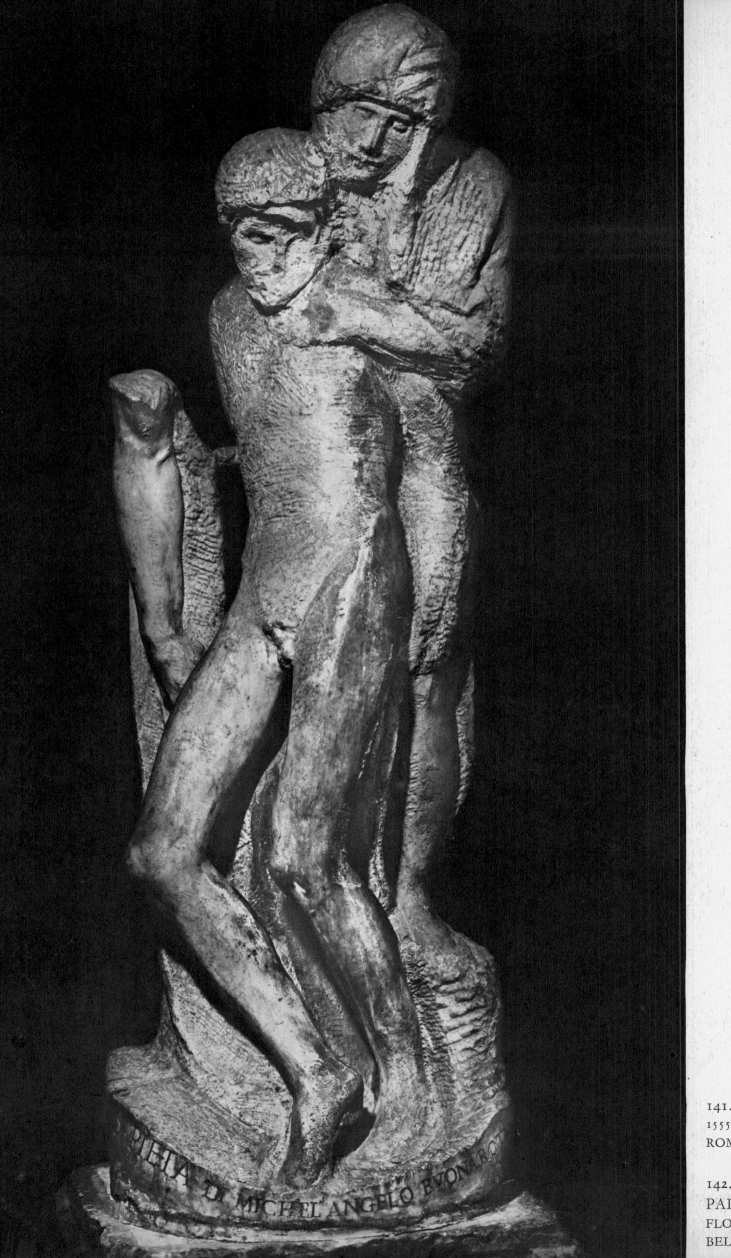

141. PIETÀ RONDANINI.
1555-1564.
ROME, PALAZZO RONDANINI

142. (opposite page) PIETÀ
PALESTRINA. AFTER 1555.
FLORENCE, ACCADEMIA DI
BELLE ARTI

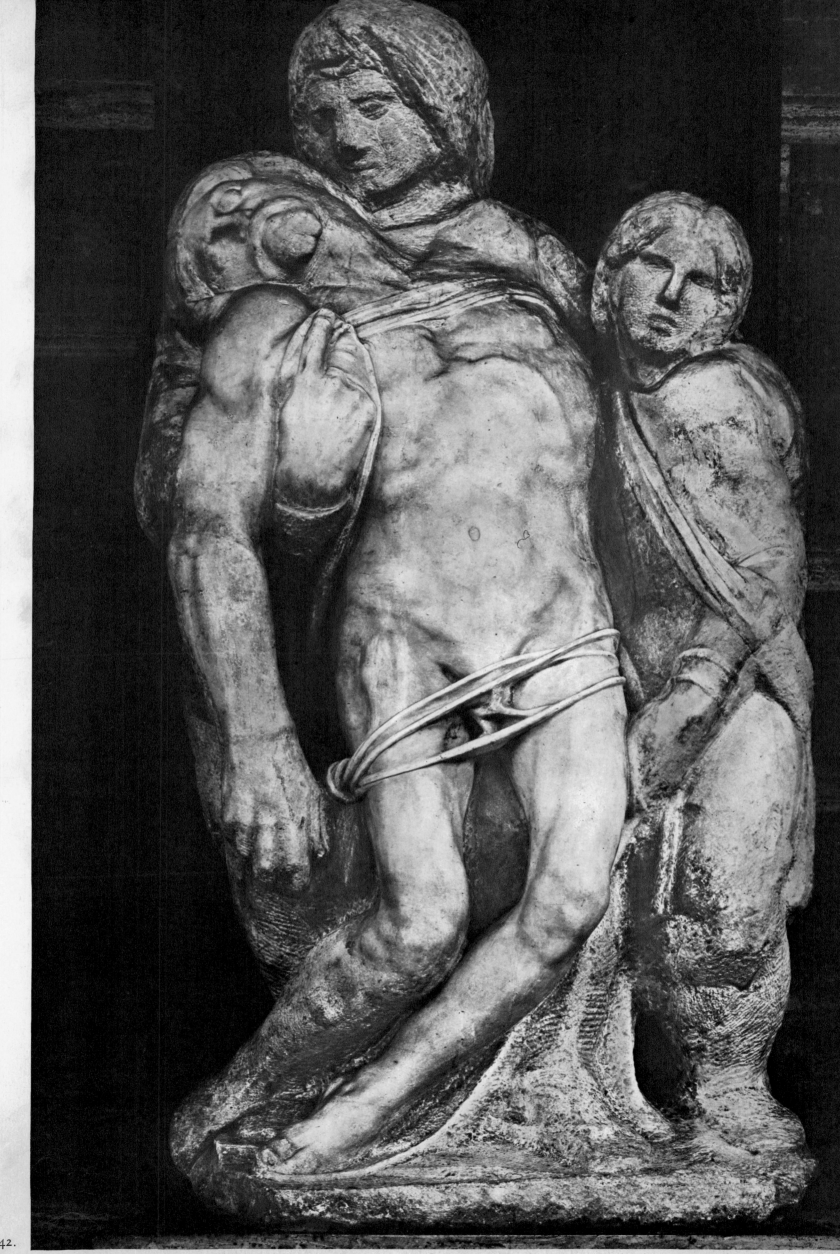

142.

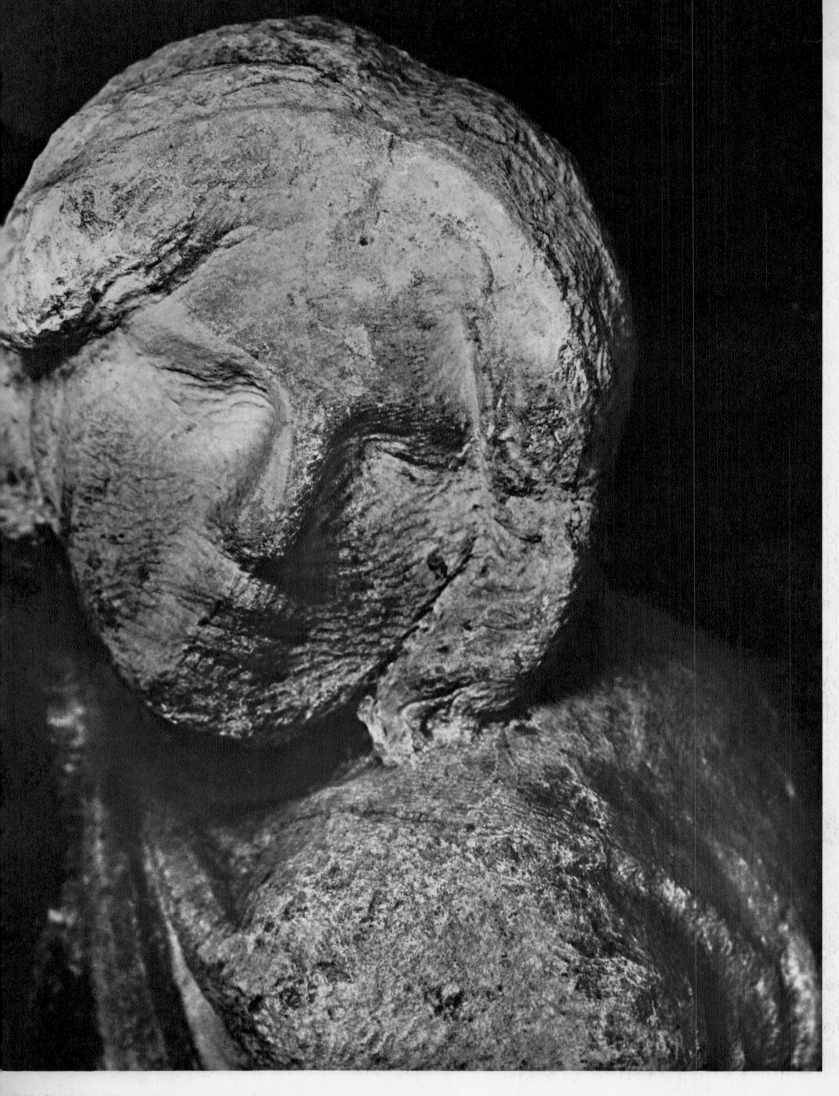

HEAD OF THE VIRGIN MARY. DETAIL FROM PLATE 142

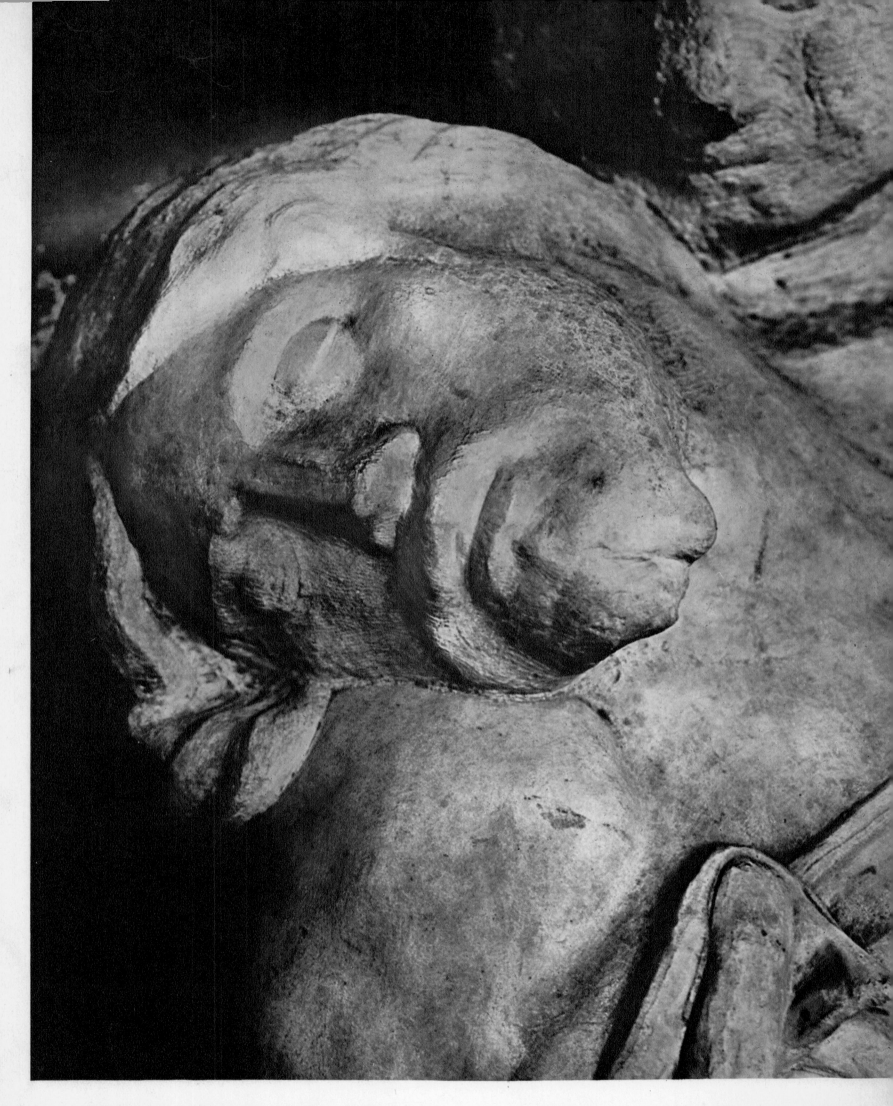

144. HEAD OF CHRIST. DETAIL FROM PLATE 142

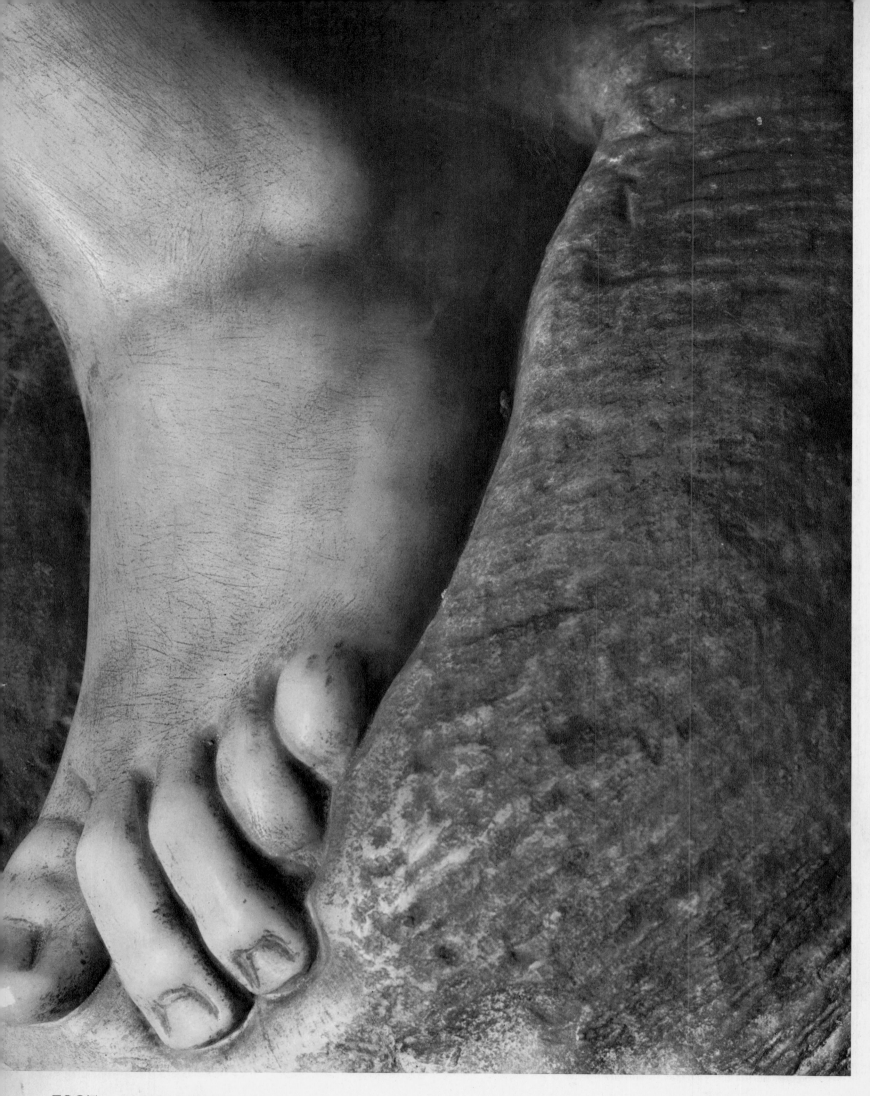

145. FOOT. DETAIL FROM PLATE 103

CONTENTS

CONTENTS

14